BROAD STREET
BIRMINGHAM

NORMAN BARTLAM

INTRODUCTION BY CARL CHINN

SUTTON PUBLISHING

Sutton Publishing Limited
Phoenix Mill · Thrupp · Stroud
Gloucestershire · GL5 2BU

First published 2002

Reprinted in 2002

Title page photograph: People who trotted
along Broad Street in 1998 would have
seen this sign, which was, however, only
publicity relating to a veterinary congress at
the International Convention Centre. But
Broad Street *was* once called Pig Lane.

British Library Cataloguing in Publication Data
A catalogue record for this book is available from the
British Library.

ISBN 0-7509-2874-3

Typeset in 10.5/13.5 Photina.
Typesetting and origination by
Sutton Publishing Limited.
Printed and bound in England by
J.H. Haynes & Co. Ltd, Sparkford.

The Prince of Wales Theatre and the Crown pub viewed through the royal arch outside the waterworks offices on the occasion of a royal visit to Birmingham, 1909.

CONTENTS

The area at the corner of Broad Street and Easy Hill as it looked in 1922. At this time the buildings were boarded up ready for demolition to be replaced by the Hall of Memory. The end building was a chemical apparatus factory. Another was the works of J.S. Nettlefold. His screw manufactory grew up with the help of his brother-in-law Joseph Chamberlain, father of the Rt Hon. Joseph Chamberlain MP. The business became a major Birmingham employer, Guest Keen & Nettlefold.

Two children collecting for the Cinderella Club which met at Oozells Street School (see p. 57).

INTRODUCTION

Broad Street today is viewed by many as the flagship street of Birmingham's regeneration and of its shift towards the service industries. The focus of the city's night life, each Friday and Saturday night Broad Street is heaving with young people parading up and down and going to and from pubs and bars in a manner reminiscent of their counterparts in Spain, Italy and southern France. Noisy, rumbustious and exhilarating, on a weekend Broad Street seems to be the 'happening' centre of Birmingham. That feeling of action is enhanced by the people who are pulled in not by the chance of good times in drinking establishments but by the variety of facilities on offer along Broad Street and its offshoots such as Brindleyplace. There is an abundance of hotels, restaurants and attractions such as Centenary Square, the International Convention Centre, Symphony Hall, the National Indoor Arena, the Birmingham Repertory Theatre and the National Sea Life Centre.

Whether you wish to enjoy classical music, Disney on Ice, Irish singers, rock bands, good food, entertaining plays, marine life or trips along the canal then Broad Street is the magnet that will draw you in. And the street is just as successful at pulling folk in from outside Birmingham and the West Midlands through its emphasis on the business, tourism and convention industries. A symbol of the revitalisation of Birmingham in the 1990s, following the marked economic downturn in the 1980s, Broad Street has stretched the city centre westwards, taking it across the Inner Ring Road and down as far as Five Ways and the borders with Edgbaston.

There can be no denying that Broad Street and Brindleyplace have energised Birmingham in general and a formerly neglected district in particular. Still, there are problems associated with the manner in which the street has been reawakened. Within just a few hundred yards lie streets in Ladywood and Lee Bank – now renamed Attwood Green – where unemployment is rife, where poverty is rampant and where hopes, dreams and expectations are crushed by the burdens of deprivation. Surely the people of Ladywood and Lee Bank should not be excluded from enjoying the facilities of Broad Street? Surely action should be taken to ensure that the wealth generated by Broad Street is shared more equally?

And if we need to include all Brummies in the success of Broad Street, then we must also recognise that the modern Broad Street did not suddenly burst into life in the late twentieth century. Like any other place, Broad Street today must be embedded within the context of its past. It is essential that the history of Broad Street and the streets that lie off it are allowed to speak of their history. How many people are aware that before Cadbury's relocated to Bournville the chocolate company was based in Bridge Street? How many of us realise that Osler's of Broad Street created one of the wonders of the Great Exhibition of 1851, a beautiful crystal fountain that struck awe into each and every person who beheld it? And how many people know of the hard times endured by so many Brummies in streets like Sheepcote Street – hard times recounted so vividly by Helen Butcher in *The Treacle Stick* (Quercus, 1999).

In our desire to catch hold of the future, we should never ignore the present nor forget the past. That is the power of this book. Through his writing, Norman Bartlam brings to the fore a Broad Street that has disappeared and in so doing he alerts us to the need to understand that Broad Street's present cannot be separated from its past.

Carl Chinn

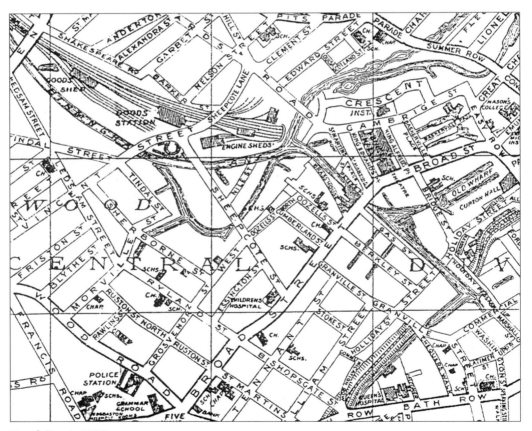

Broad Street, 1907.

1

Around Centenary Square

Old meets new. One of the statues at the Hall of Memory looks away from the gleaming new Hyatt Regency Hotel, July 1991.

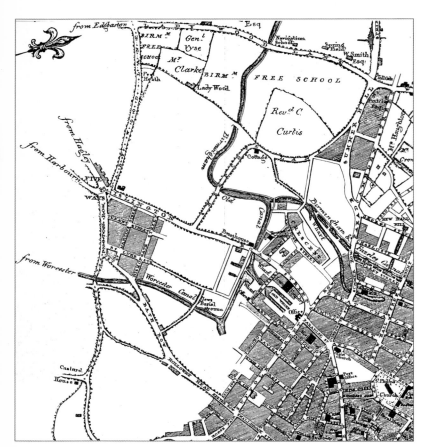

Kempson's map of 1810 shows the town of Birmingham extending out to Broad Street around the canal junction at Old Wharf. The Crescent was an early attempt to provide upmarket residential development that had fine panoramic views of the rolling countryside towards Summerhill and Ladywood. There was a cluster of development around Five Ways. This end of Broad Street was at that time called Islington; historian William Hutton described it as a 'hamlet belonging to Birmingham'.

This was the Bath-like crescent of twenty-three houses as it appeared in an architect's vision in the late 1780s. The Napoleonic Wars and the continued expansion of the town somewhat curtailed the scheme, and only the buildings on the left were put up. The rapid appearance of factories and smoky chimneys somehow did not appeal to the yuppies of the 1780s. In 1924 a theatre group was established here and their first act was to name themselves the Crescent Theatre. The theatre is now located in Brindleyplace. Thomas Attwood, the City's first MP, lived in one of the buildings.

John Baskerville (1706–75) became a well-known printer; he was the type of person who would be recognised. In 1745 he built his home in 8 acres of land on what was at the time the fringe of the town: this is where Centenary Square now stands. His typeface became popular with printers, and in 1757 a book of Virgil's poems printed with his typeface 'went forth to astonish the librarians of Europe'. Baskerville became the printer at Cambridge University, hence Cambridge Street, which runs behind Broad Street.

Baskerville flouted convention, this in the days before the Convention Centre, and held anti-religious views. He chose to be buried upright in a tomb in his back garden. Some years later the tomb was excavated during the construction of a series of canals and dubious and curious Brummies reportedly paid 6*d* per head to gawp at the corpse, which was put on display in a warehouse. They had much to see, for in spite of being in a state of rest for forty-six years, the body's skin was said to be 'dry, but perfect, the eyes were gone but the eyebrows, lips, and teeth remained'. The *Birmingham Gazette* reported that after a while the corpse gave off 'an exceedingly offensive and oppressive effluvia strongly resembling decayed cheese'. He was eventually laid to rest in Christ Church at Victoria Square, but later removed when the church was demolished, and is now in Warstone Lane Cemetery at Hockley.

After Baskerville's death another local wealthy businessman, John Ryland, purchased the house, but it was burned down during the Priestley Riots of 1791. A number of rioters who had apparently become drunk on the contents of the cellar were consumed in the flames.

The land where Baskerville had his house was eventually sold off, and an arm of the canal from Wolverhampton was dug into the area where Centenary Square now stands. Baskerville Wharf was one of many wharves where coal was unloaded for the factories along the street. This advertisement dates from 1910 when coal sold at 8d per cwt.

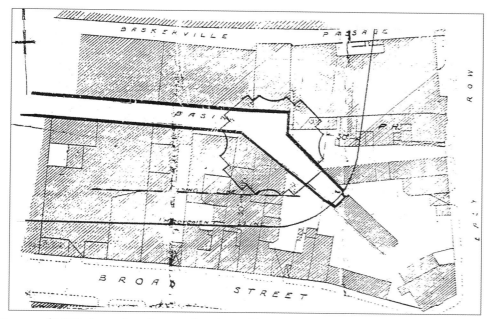

This map of 1922 shows the aforementioned canal basin with the outline of the soon to be erected Hall of Memory superimposed on it. Most of the surrounding land was cleared and the canals filled in. In 1935 an architectural competition was held to design the municipal blocks that were planned for the site. Only one was built and this became Baskerville House.

The Prince of Wales conducted the stone-laying ceremony for the Hall of Memory on 12 June 1923. He used a silver trowel with an ivory handle to tap the stone neatly into place. Inside the hall, a book of remembrance lists all local people killed in conflicts throughout the world. On the day it opened in 1925 30,000 people queued to pay their respects.

Two of the four bronze statues that now sit on the outer walls of the Hall of Memory. The one on the left represents the army and the other the air force. The two other sculptures represent the navy and the nursing service. They were designed by Birmingham-born sculptor Albert Toft.

The Hall of Memory hosts the Armistice Day celebrations, *c.* 1926. A Portland stone colonnade shielded the adjacent Gardens of Rest from the nearby factories. It was removed during the construction of Centenary Square in 1990 and rebuilt in a Peace Garden at St Thomas' Church, near Five Ways. The land on the right had been cleared for the building of the new Civic Centre. Industrial giant R.W. Winfield's occupied one of the buildings, which was also removed.

Part of the Hall of Memory can just be seen on the left of this photograph, which shows an Admiralty inspection on 15 April 1944. The magnificent buildings in the background are on Easy Row, and they were demolished to be replaced by an office block and hotel of little architectural merit.

This view of the Hall of Memory and gardens was taken in 1957. It also shows Baskerville House, a council building erected on the site of John Baskerville's house. It was the only one of a number of similar buildings planned to form a major civic centre. Baskerville House is now being converted into a hotel, which will open in 2003. In the gardens stands a fountain built to commemorate the completion of the Elan Valley Aqueduct, which carries Birmingham's water supply from Wales.

The Repertory Theatre and part of Centenary Square now occupy the land where this line of buildings once stood. The 1947 view from Bridge Street was made possible by enemy action, which destroyed numerous buildings in the area. The tall white building was the home of a long line of surgeons, the most famous being Joseph Sampson Gamgee. Adjacent to it stood a cigar and stamp shop, which was said to be the smallest shop in Birmingham at the time of its closure in 1933. The building on the right belonged to Messenger's, a leading manufacturer of chandeliers, candelabra and brass fittings, which may have been established as early as 1747. In 1884 Messenger's, together with nearby Bolton's, produced 16,000 miles of copper wire, which formed part of the first Atlantic telegraph cable. From the 1930s this block was home to the Hungry Man Restaurant.

Joseph Sampson Gamgee (1828–86) was a pioneering surgeon. He founded the Hospital Saturday Fund movement, whereby workers donated their earnings on one Saturday a year to a special fund. This raised money to build an extension to Queen's Hospital, which became the world-famous Accident Hospital. Gamgee is credited with inventing Gamgee Tissues and artificial sponges, a prototype cotton wool dressing. Author J.R.R.Tolkien, who was brought up in Birmingham, adopted the name of Gamgee in his novels *The Hobbit* and *The Lord of the Rings*.

The Repertory Theatre stands on the site of Gamgee's house. The theatre, opened in 1971, is seen here in an unusual view as Symphony Hall and the ICC entrance take shape in April 1988. The award-winning theatre replaced a smaller one in Station Street in the city centre, which was established thanks to the efforts of Sir Barry Jackson (1879–1961), founder of the Birmingham Repertory Company. Its first production was *First Impressions*, a musical adaptation of *Pride and Prejudice*.

February 1990 saw the end of the gardens as we knew them. The Colonnades, by then a dirty rundown eyesore, were removed and later restored and re-erected in a peace garden near Five Ways. The fountain and a line of benches were also removed to make way for the largest open square to be built in Europe since the Second World War. It was planned in 1989, a hundred years after Birmingham achieved city status, and so became known as Centenary Square. At the same time the ring road, which cut the area off from the city centre, was lowered to create a surface level, people-friendly crossing from the city to Broad Street.

Centenary Square was laid out in 525,000 brick paviors to a design that resembles a Persian carpet. The square quickly established itself as a major venue for the performing arts. In the weeks leading up to the official opening of the ICC over fifty saxophonists in spacesuits abseiled down the Hyatt Regency Hotel; 20,000 walkers converged on it for a walkathon; a symbolic ring-giving ceremony inspired by the Jewellery Quarter was held; and a heat of Britain's best-known bicycle race, the Milk Race, started and finished here.

This statue is the centrepiece of the Square. It is called 'Forward' (the city's motto), and records the changing economy of the city from an industrial manufacturing giant to a forward-looking business and tourism orientated economy. Designed by local-born sculptor Raymond Mason, the 26 ft long structure is made of polychrome resin. The proud taller figures at the front look forward to the future, facing the ICC. The lady behind them is blowing a kiss to the industrial past. Traditional Birmingham industries are depicted as the characters disappear into history and the darker colours signify the grimy industrial past. On one side a schoolteacher leads his pupils to a brighter future and notable city figures, Neville, Austen and Joseph Chamberlain, can be seen. The actress looks towards the theatre and a musician towards Symphony Hall. At various angles people can be seen reaching for the future. A chemical symbol recalls the pioneering work undertaken on DNA at Birmingham University. A motor car signifies the work of Herbert Austin, who developed a prototype car while working for the Wolseley Sheep Shearing Company on Broad Street. When it was unveiled the statue was likened to a pink blancmange but is now generally recognised as a major work of art and talking point.

Drunken locals leaving the Cambridge Inn in 1938 may have slept off their drink and woken up believing that they had seen a dinosaur walking by, and they'd have been right! This is Egbert breathing out clouds of smoke as he leaves the workshop where he was made on Cambridge Street. He was a central character in Birmingham's Centenary celebrations for the granting of its charter of incorporation in 1838, which were held in Aston Park. Behind him stands the well-known and long-established Upton printing works.

Cambridge Street behind the ICC, 1930. The central building is the Prince of Wales pub, which was built in 1854 and named after the nearby theatre, which was in turn named after the Prince. In 1984 plans were drawn up to demolish it, but regular customers fought off the planners and it has twice recently been named Birmingham's pub of the year. Sadly the customers' loyalty was not repaid because the traditional pub was, in what was described as 'legalised vandalism', completely revamped and its interior and character destroyed. Bingley Hall can be seen on the far left. Nearby stood the industrial firm of R.W. Winfield's, which exhibited at the Great Exhibition of 1851 in London.

The City Council lighting depot on Cambridge Street, 1 January 1986. The gas lamplighters were based here. Initially certain residents of the town of Birmingham took a dim view of street lighting and opposed the introduction of it, fearing that it might induce crime! Lamps burning whale oil, which was bought from Hull for 3s 4d a gallon, once lit up much of the town. Eventually William Murdoch's 'gas illumination' became popular.

The site of the lighting depot and surrounding land was turned into a city centre garden. Pupils from nearby Nelson School worked with residents from the tower blocks to contribute to its design. They are pictured with Councillor Pat Sever who was chair of the Convention Centre committee, headteacher Mike Ryan, the class teacher and the author of this book, Norman Bartlam.

2

The Site of the International Convention Centre

The site of the ICC, October 1983. Most of the site was occupied by Bingley Hall. Gas Street canal basin is at the bottom. On the left of the photograph can be seen the canal, which was dug into a deep cutting across the Broad Street ridge. The wall was eventually demolished and the land where the triangular car park is was excavated to canal level. This created a dramatic canalside entrance when the ICC was built. The Brewmaster's House stands at one corner of the triangle by the canal wall, and still stands today.

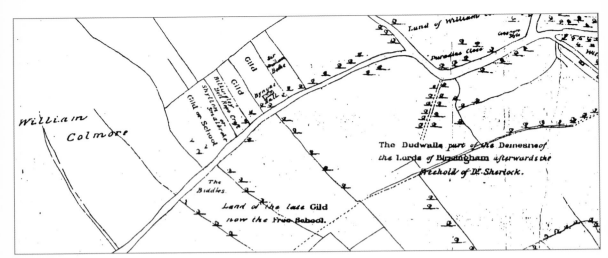

A map of the area dated 1553. Broad Street was just a lane running across the map. The road leading off it on the left to the top of the map became Sheepcote Street, which today forms the boundary of Brindleyplace. The ICC now covers most of the area around where Byngas Hall once stood. On the right the road divides land owned by the Colmore and Sherlock families. The curve in the road still exists, and Paradise Close is now Paradise Circus.

Byngas Hall, which was built in about 1760 and later became Bingley Hall, was the home of James Farmer. It stood where the ICC now stands. Mr Farmer's daughter married Charles Lloyd, son of the banker Sampson Lloyd, and they subsequently lived at the house. In 1883 the local press described it as having lawns on which were kept rabbits, 'who seem to enjoy their freedom'. The house was said to be 'an old-fashioned house of the grange, or superior country clergyman style'. The grounds of Bingley Hall were used for a temporary exhibition of Birmingham wares in 1849 and Prince Albert, one of the visitors, was so impressed that he went away to conceive the idea of the Great Exhibition of 1851, an early example of London following in Birmingham's footsteps. A fund was established to raise money for a permanent hall. By 1850 enough money had been raised to build what was to become Birmingham's first purpose-built exhibition centre, pre-dating the ICC by 140 years!

Bingley Hall was the scene of a mass rally to celebrate the seventieth birthday of Joseph Chamberlain in July 1906. The hall was often used for political events, and it is thought that a speech there by Gladstone in 1888 was the first to be recorded on Edison's newly invented phonograph, brought from the United States.

This advertisement for Bingley Hall skating rink dates from 1876. It is recorded that 'for a time, the amusement was exceedingly popular with more than one fortunate accruing from the manufacture of roller skates'. In 1878 a Mr Betteridge got his skates on and travelled 200 miles in twenty-four hours around the hall. For a time circuses were also popular events. A performer apparently once 'danced gracefully on a tightrope, whilst wearing skates'.

Edgbaston and Ladywood Advertister and Literary Repository.

BINGLEY HALL SKATING RINKS,

(Entrance in King Edward's Place), Broad Street, Birmingham.

THE CELEBRATED

Plimpton's Patent Roller Skates,

Same as used at Prince's Club, Brompton, &c., &c.

THESE SPACIOUS RINKS WILL BE OPEN DAILY,

(Sundays, and such other days as may be necessary in consequence of Agricultural Shows, &c., excepted).

MORNING CLASSES from 11 a.m. to 1 p.m.   AFTERNOON ASSEMBLIES from 2-30 p.m. to 5 p.m.   EVENING ASSEMBLIES from 7 p.m. to 10 p.m.   A first-class BAND in attendance each Evening, and Wednesday and Saturday Afternoons.

Admission, One Shilling; Children under 12, Sixpence.

HIRE OF SKATES, SIXPENCE.

BOOKS, containing 25 ADMISSION TICKETS, £1 1s. 0d.   Ditto for Children, 10s.6d.   BOOKS containing 25 SKATE TICKETS, 10s.6d.

SEASON TICKETS are issued for 3, 6, or 12 months on liberal terms.

Lavatories, Cloak Rooms, Waiting Room supplied with Morning, Evening, and Comic Papers, and every convenience for Visitors, Skaters, or Non-Skaters.

During September, MONTHLY SEASON TICKETS, to include use of Skates, and available AT ALL TIMES when the Rinks are open, will be issued at One Guinea each.

HENRY GREEN, Manager.

Many thousands of Brummies will have visited circuses, cattle shows and concerts during the building's 134-year history, most without incident. In 1896, though, a lion escaped from a menagerie while the electric light was turned off. She attacked a horse and was shot while devouring it. The correspondence written on the back of this postcard, date-stamped 1908, reads: 'would you believe it is 5s to go in'.

In later years Bingley Hall was famous as the venue for the Midland Ideal Home Exhibitions. In 1984 the hall was destroyed by a fire which wrecked the Midlands Caravan, Camping & Leisure Exhibition, which had opened only days before. The managing director of the company that leased the hall from the City Council was Tony Bullimore, who became famous for his round-the-world yachting exploits. The local press reported: 'Birmingham's famous Bingley Hall was built in just six weeks and badly damaged in only sixty minutes.'

The entrance to Bingley Hall (and now the ICC) was on King Alfred's Place, and this is how it looked at the junction with Cambridge Street in 1920. The occupiers were timber merchants called D.T. Powell, who later moved to the railway sidings in Ladywood.

The interior of the Prince of Wales Theatre was destroyed during the Second World War, but the façade remains in this 1948 view of the building, which stands in front of Bingley Hall. The Church of the Messiah stood over the canal. A bus travelling into the city centre is passing the junction of King Edward's Place at the Crown public house. Next to the theatre stands the Broadway Café, although it was better known by its former name of The Towrope. Binney's the mill furnishers had a long-established business here. The Brasshouse can be seen in the distance.

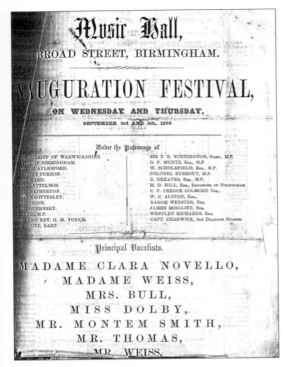

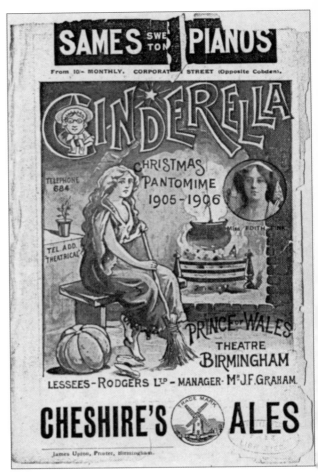

The Prince of Wales Theatre began life as a music hall and operetta house, a high-class music venue that opened in 1856. In spite of having the second largest organ in England its notes failed to reach the ears of Brummies and it was closed. It reopened as the 'most complete elegant theatre in the provinces', adopting the name of Prince of Wales to commemorate the wedding of the future Edward VII. It was reconstructed in 1876 and pantomimes were held on a regular basis. Once during a performance of *Tarzan* a real lion was used. Planks on which the cage was suspended gave way, leaving the lion hovering over the orchestra pit! The theatre had a fine record and was much loved by the playgoing public until the interior was destroyed by enemy action on 9 April 1941. The outer façade remained until it was demolished to make way for the ICC.

The ICC now stands on this site. (Compare this with the view on p. 34.) The large building in the centre is the former brewery store behind the Crown pub. To the right of it stands the site of the now-demolished Bingley Hall and Prince of Wales theatre. The paved area in the bottom left is the site of the Church of the Messiah. Next to it stands the timbered Stratford House antique shop at the head of a triangle of roads, which are shown on the map below. The car park on the triangle was the site of another church, St Peter's. On the extreme left is the Brewmaster's House. By 1980 over 40 per cent of the land was either derelict or used for car parking.

This 1888 map shows the triangle of roads that can be seen above. St Peter's Church, burial ground and school covered most of the triangle. A line of cottages on St Martin's Place had, at that time, neat little gardens. The square building next to the towpath is the Brewmaster's House and behind it is the malthouse, which had a private canal basin. Today the entrance to that basin can be seen on the canalside adjacent to the appropriately named Malthouse pub. The Sunday school hall was part of the Church of the Messiah, which was built on arches above the canal. It later featured in the Cliff Richard film *Take Me High*, when it became a club selling 'Brumburgers'! The superimposed thick black line shows the outer edge of where the ICC was built. The spot marking the canalside entrance to the Mall was originally about 20 ft beneath ground level in the burial ground. There is always somebody about to direct you!

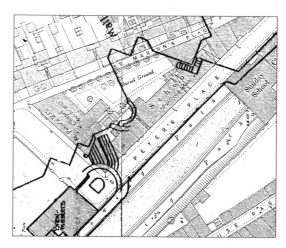

These cottages on St Martin's Place were built in about 1800. In 1847 a railway company bought 'the substrata lying and being under' some of the cottages for the 'purpose to excavate by blasting with gunpowder if necessary' a tunnel for the Birmingham–Wolverhampton railway. The railway line still exists, and part of the ICC building has soundproofing in the foundations to eliminate noise and vibration from the trains beneath. It is thought that St Martin's Place was so called because a ropemaker who lived there made the bell ropes for St Martin's Church in the Bull Ring. Another suggestion is that twine, used in the manufacture of the ropes, was grown here and that, in a case of money for old rope, some of the cottages may have been built using cash from a bell rope trust. This area became a conservation area in 1969 and there were plans to turn it into a street museum.

This is the other side of the triangle of roads that is shown on the map on the previous page. The road is St Peter's Place, showing St Peter's School shortly before demolition in October 1969. Brewmaster's House can just be seen on the extreme left. The canal is in the foreground in the cutting. St Peter's Church can be seen in the middle. The land where the school had stood was excavated to canal level, allowing pedestrian access from the ICC to the canalside.

St Peter's Roman Catholic Church and Presbytery shortly before demolition in November 1969. St Martin's Place runs down the left. The church opened in 1786 although it was not consecrated until the building debts were paid off in 1933. It was built to look a little like a factory and many people were surprised that it was a church – a case of 'Phew, it's a pew!' These were still the days of bitter religious prejudice, and it was better not to attract too much attention to it.

A 1956 wedding at St Peter's Church, with the cottages on St Martin's Row in the background. The wedding couple are Nora Wilson and Frank Bartlam, the parents of the author of this book. The church closed in 1969.

The Brewmaster's House as it looked *c.* 1850. It was probably built earlier that century for the manager of the brewery, which stands behind it. It was then called the Birmingham Brewery and should not be confused with the Crown Brewery, which stood nearby. A report stated: 'several Birmingham gentlemen decided that it would be to the convenience of the inhabitants of the town if a public brewery was erected to supply them with ale, porter and beer of genuine quality and at a moderate price'. There were no hiccups in the plan and the first drink was served in about 1814.

The Brewmaster's House stands in splendid isolation on 15 March 1987 as demolition work continues ahead of the building of the ICC. The land clearance included the removal of the graveyard of St Peter's Church: 1,163 bodies were removed from the site even though the church records indicated the presence of only 577. The additional bodies were thought to have been buried quickly because of a rapidly spreading disease. Some suggest it may have been the plague, while others think the area is, maybe, plagued by a myth, and the disease was cholera. The bodies were re-interred at Oscott cemetery.

A 1986 view of the Brewmaster's House, looking along the canal towards Broad Street. The tall wall which enclosed the canal was demolished and the land behind it, where the graveyard was, was removed to open up the canalside. The empty brewery building stands near the Brewmaster's House; this was soon to disappear, to be replaced by the ICC.

The same view, April 1993. A canal layby was dug in March 1990 to enable narrow boats to moor up at the ICC, so that delegates and tourists could be taken on trips around the revitalised canal network. This is a popular tour in summer and people queue up here for a tour of the network.

The Broad Street corner of the triangle showing the former Three Horseshoes pub, which later became known as the Stratford House antique shop, in the centre. At this time, 1938, a plumber's merchant occupied it. Gittins' was a well-known electrical dealer. The church on the left was the Church of the Messiah. The cyclist is on St Peter's Place heading towards the Brewmaster's House. The other street is St Martin's Place. Most of the area on the right is now the vehicle entrance and loading bay for the ICC.

The area around the Stratford House antique shop was at the time of demolition a thriving antique area. This 'N' That collectors' shop was on St Martin's Place next to Stratford House. This picture was on the front of the City Council's publicity brochure that encouraged people to stay in the Big Heart of England. It was still being used after the heart had been ripped out of the area in 1986.

This marvellous row of Georgian buildings, pictured in May 1986, stood at the junction of King Alfred's Place and Broad Street. Mr Lindner established an export company there in 1888. He became the German consul and 'confided the interests of that vast continental empire in its relation with the trades of Birmingham. A more Honourable position could not be desired by a businessman.' Thomas Smith had a well-known violin shop which stood next to the Celebrity Restaurant. For a number of years these buildings were under threat of demolition, and there was an outcry from conservationists when the announcement was finally made that consent for this had been granted. At a public inquiry the Victorian Society complained that not enough had been done to integrate old buildings into the new design. The Environment Minister, in giving the go-ahead, said the redevelopment project was 'an exciting and impressive project, which provides a great opportunity to create a more prosperous city'.

King Alfred's Place was built on land owned by the King Edward's Foundation and named after the King of Wessex. This view of the entrance to the ICC and façade of Symphony Hall was taken in July 1991 at the same spot as the photograph above. Which of the two views do you prefer?

The Crown public house was established in 1781 when fields surrounded it and Broad Street was still called Pig Lane, so presumably the drinkers were dis-grunt-led when they trotted out at closing time. Behind it was built a huge brewery, the chimneys of which date from 1880.

The Crown in June 1989, during construction of the ICC. Notice the end wall of the pub as it looked before a Georgian reproduction façade was erected. As part of a revamp the historic interior was destroyed and artefacts, including a turn-of-the-century grandfather clock, were removed. In what was seen by many as an unbelievable act of stupidity the name of the historic pub was changed to Edward's.

Mr William Butler is the man most closely associated with the Crown. In 1843 he came from his Leicestershire home to look for employment and found it at a hairdresser's near the pub. He eventually married the sister of the Crown's proprietor and after a while took over the pub, thereby completing a move from the crown of the head to the head of the Crown! He later joined forces with Mr Henry Mitchell at Cape Hill to form Mitchell & Butler's brewery. It is said that the company logo, a leaping deer, signifies the sights that could be seen as Butler walked over the fields of Ladywood between the two establishments.

The ceremonial demolition of a wall by Councillor Pat Sever, chairman of the ICC Committee, in July 1986 was followed by the removal of the first sod of earth from the site in May 1987. Within weeks this large hole appeared as work began to remove over 320,000 cu. ft of sandstone from the Broad Street ridge to make way for the foundations of Symphony Hall. The tower blocks in the distance are on Cambridge Street.

The Crown, as work began on pile driving for the foundations of Symphony Hall. Eventually, in a carefully orchestrated move, 1,500 tons of structural steelwork and 7,000 tons of steel reinforcements were erected to form the frame of the building. During renovation work on the pub a 65 ft deep well was unearthed. Experts looked into it, and said 'Well, well, well, I think it dates from the sixteenth century.'

The ICC takes shape around the Crown in 1989. The steelwork is the roof of Symphony Hall: in early plans the hall was to have been erected nearer the canal, which meant the Crown was in the way of the development. Plans were drawn up to move it on special hydraulic jacks to a site a few yards away, but the plans were altered because of the costs involved. From the canalside a walkway through the ICC, which was to become the Mall, is taking shape.

An October 1988 view of the Broad Street side of Symphony Hall with the Crown public house in the background. The advert claims it will become one of the world's great concert halls. Compare this view with the same view in 1948 on p. 23. A fact that will be music to trivia freaks is that Symphony Hall was built with over 180,000 cu. ft of concrete. Apparently that's enough to fill 518 double-decker buses – that's a lot of concrete and a lot of dirty buses!

The Mall takes shape in April 1989. It became a 403 ft long central corridor to the ICC, with a roof made of 1,640 sq. ft of solar controlled glass supported by stainless steel rods. During a visit to the site in November 1987 Prince Charles said he thought the development looked like 'a concrete missile silo'.

Pupils from Ladywood School, under the direction of the school's head of geography and author of this book, took a keen interest in the development of the Broad Street Redevelopment Area and made a number of video programmes showing progress of the area. Here the film crew record the installation of the Hyatt Hotel bridge link on a Sunday morning in February 1989. Pictured are Brendan Brogan, Daniel Millward and Mark Bartlett.

Symphony Hall contains 2,211 seats and is the home of the City of Birmingham Symphony Orchestra. Although the hall was built as a classical music venue it has staged all types of music and performances. Special guests have included Nelson Mandela. The hall itself was the single most expensive part of the ICC, costing £35 million. The final part of the hall was not completed until autumn 2001, when an organ was added in a £1.3 million project. The total cost of the ICC, including Symphony Hall, was around £180 million.

This is the reverberation chamber beneath Symphony Hall, proving that inside it may resemble a nineteenth-century concert hall but that there is nothing old-fashioned about it at all. Noise and vibration from the nearby railway is absorbed by this series of 675 rubber pads built into the foundations in a 12 ft deep chamber. Inside the building state-of-the-art technology enables sound to be adjusted by using reverberation chambers, control banners and an adjustable canopy above the stage.

The ICC building holds not only Symphony Hall but also ten other halls for meetings; the largest fixed seat hall has 1,500 seats. These halls are reached by escalator from the mall and are usually out of bounds to the general public.

Children from local schools helped to unveil the foundation stone at the ICC canalside entrance, although it had been officially used at a ceremony to launch the project a few years earlier when the European Commission paid a visit. Inside the stone there are, among other things, a pair of ballet shoes, a signed Aston Villa football and a gold ring made in the nearby Jewellery Quarter. The Ladywood Consortium of Schools played an important part in helping to capture the hearts and minds of local people during the building of the ICC, through the enthusiastic efforts of ICC Committee Chairman Pat Sever and schools liaison officer Norman Bartlam. Local residents were kept informed via a video news programme shown at regular meetings in a portakabin on the ICC site (see p. 35).

The Queen officially opened the ICC on 12 June 1991, although the first convention was held in April 1991. The city's Lord Mayor at the time was Councillor Bill Turner, who lives in nearby Ladywood. During her visit the Queen opened a congress of the International Olympic Committee.

Local residents of Ladywood met the Queen when she opened the ICC. Here Edie Ockford, who has lived locally all her life, shakes hands with her. Edie says: 'I was delighted that "ordinary" people of Ladywood could get to meet her. It was a most fantastic day and one that I will remember for the rest of my life.'

When the Queen reached the registration area of the ICC she was met by three hundred children from twenty local schools, who sang a specially composed song, 'I am the Child of The City'.

On the day of the royal opening children from the Oratory Primary School formed a guard of honour at the statue and parted as the Queen arrived. The sculptor, Raymond Mason, is standing near the statue behind the school's headteacher, Frank Farrell.

Children from St Patrick's RC Primary School fly the European Union flag to launch the European leaders' summit at the ICC in October 1992. The local press stated: 'This is what the ICC was built for, and city councillors behind the scheme never had any doubt they were building the best in Europe.' Around five thousand delegates and journalists attended the event.

The most prestigious event so far held at the ICC was the world leaders' G8 Summit in 1989. US President Bill Clinton went on a walkabout and visited the canalside pub the Malthouse. The publicity this brought to the city was enormous, and the summit was heavily featured on the TV news in this country and abroad.

In its first ten years the ICC has hosted 4,000 events and 1.5 million people have visited the building. The largest convention was the Lions International Congress, which was held in June 1998 and included a ceremonial march-past along Broad Street.

In 1996 one of the chefs at the International Convention Centre, Scott O'Hara, won a prestigious award for this sugar barn owl, which was used as a centrepiece on a banqueting table. It was made from 30 lb of icing sugar, mixed with egg whites, glycerine and cornflour, and the completed owl contains over 1,000 individually sculptured feathers. The rat was the most difficult piece to complete; Scott made eighty claws of different shapes and sizes before deciding on those for the final sculpture. Other examples of the kitchen chef's work can be seen in the ICC Mall.

All of the main halls at the ICC have fixed seating but Hall Three can be used for exhibitions. The roof supports are strong enough to support heavy displays, including articulated lorries. Visitors can, if so inclined, view the underside and admire the suspension of the vehicle.

The ICC and Centenary Square, September 1999. Preparations are under way in the square for a music concert as part of the BBC Music Fest. On the right an extension to the Repertory Theatre is nearing completion. To the left stands the Hyatt Regency Hotel, linked to the ICC by a bridge. Behind the main ICC building can be seen the Brindleyplace development and the National Indoor Arena (NIA).

3

Around Brindleyplace

An aerial view of Brindleyplace with the ICC to the top left, June 1999. Symphony Court (a triangle of housing) and Sheepcote Street are in the bottom left.

The Unitarian Church of the Messiah was built over the canal in January 1862 and it is pictured here three years after opening. It was said that baptisms were held by opening a trap door and dunking the unsuspecting babies in the canal! Joseph Chamberlain was a member of the congregation. The church was occasionally rented out for school use. In 1876 it was recorded that 'the daily crowding of a large number of unwashed children into the rooms, the odour from whom makes the rooms so close and unpleasant produces a permanent effect on the walls of the rooms and makes them need to be thoroughly cleaned much more frequently than they would otherwise have to be to keep them fresh and wholesome and fit for our congregational purpose'. The other buildings include the hairdresser where William Butler worked before becoming a brewer and a corn dealer. The church was demolished in April 1978.

This is a scene from about 1936 showing typical forms of transport passing the Church of the Messiah. The other building is the Brasshouse. Streets are traditionally known in Birmingham as 'the 'orse road'.

A view of what is now the Brasshouse Restaurant and pub, but as the name suggests it was originally built as a brassworks. A number of local merchants were brassed off, so to speak, by the cost of brass, and 200 of them raised £100 each to erect the building in 1781. From then on they could join forces to combat the rising price of the metal. As a result of their endeavours the price of brass fell from £84 to £56 per ton. The company continued to make brass until at least 1850, and then the building was sold to the waterworks company. Today the frontage remains almost unaltered, although the central arch, which provided access for wagons to the furnaces at the rear, is now the front door for diners who like to make a meal of their history.

Brasshouse Passage ran up the side of the Brasshouse. The Brasshouse became the Weights & Measures Department, and later was used by the Samaritans and the Brasshouse adult education centre. The white building belonged to Oozells Street School. There were once a number of small houses in the passage, but these were converted to industrial use. Industrial concerns at the turn of the century included manufacturers of toys, ovens, tinplate, glass and buttons. In 1864 it is recorded that there were twelve three-storey houses with stables and outbuildings, but these were in 'a dilapidated state' and 'fit only for a very low class of tenants'. The building behind the Brasshouse was an industrial research laboratory.

On 7 July 1909 King Edward VII and Queen Alexandra opened Birmingham University, and the royal procession travelled down Broad Street. The Water Department which then owned the Brasshouse, on the extreme left, built this arch to commemorate the visit and promote the success of the Elan Valley water scheme, which had been completed five years earlier. It attracted a flood of admirers, but that is all water under the arch now!

The arch spanned the width of Broad Street and attracted huge crowds, including a line of nearly 3,000 children. The photograph below was turned into a postcard, and the handwritten message on the back reads: 'On the day of the Royal visit there was a Welsh lady stood one side of the arch and a little Welsh girl the other and when you see the ladies stand water came down there, real water, for we seen that trickling down. Very pretty it looked.' The Prince of Wales theatre was one of many buildings to be illuminated 'with either gas or electric devices, in the shape of the Royal initials, stars or coronets'. The press added: 'one pleasing feature was the erection of numerous spots of water stands. These were attached to fire hydrants on which hung a number of tin mugs. Although they were provided for the children there was no lack of application for drinks from the adults. Each stand was guarded by an official from the Water Department.'

A police call box marks the junction of St Peter's Place and Broad Street. Gittins' on the right was an electrical retailer. The Church of the Messiah stands next to the Brasshouse. Opposite can just be seen Midwinter's bakery, next to which stands Everyman, a stationery shop, and County Cycles is at the corner of Gas Street.

A famous name in the motor trade, Herbert Austin, worked for the Wolseley Sheep Shearing Machine Company near the corner of Oozells Street. For a time he worked for Wolseley in Australia and became concerned about the length of time it took to travel across the continent. On his return he set about improving methods of transport and built a prototype car in a shed at the rear of the premises. It was a two horse-powered, three-wheeled vehicle, a model of which appeared in Centenary Square in 1985 to mark Wolseley's centenary. Austin worked with Broad Street-based Mulliner coachbuilders to develop a furnace for heating tyres and wheels. Austin, Wolseley and Mulliner all became famous names.

This was an ordinary block of former factories in January 1986, illustrating how run down the street had become, but the amount of history in the block is tremendous. The building on the far right belonged to Jarrett & Rainsford, the ladies' compact makers, while nearby stood the premises of Parker, Winder & Achurch, Charles Winn, brassfounders, and G.E. Belliss & Co., all of whom achieved greatness and became household names. Oozells Street is on the left.

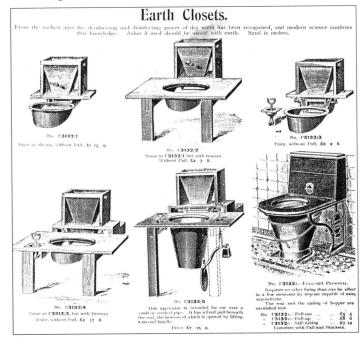

A page from Parker, Winder & Achurch's 1904 catalogue. They were leading sellers of architectural ironmongery and hardware. The closets were obviously popular: the staff had no time to sit down on the job as they were kept busy selling these essential wares; every household wanted one. William Parker established the business in 1836, and later it expanded and moved to larger premises across the road until about 1929. It moved out of Broad Street in 1972 after 136 years of trading.

In 1860, when the brass industry began to flourish on Broad Street, Jarrett & Rainsford set up business employing six men in the manufacture of brass pins. They pinned their hopes on selling to wholesale drapery and haberdashery outlets, and the business proved popular. They expanded into cosmetic jewellery and the Stratton brand of ladies' powder compacts was particularly well liked. The company outgrew the Broad Street premises and moved out in 1909. This site is now occupied by a large office block, no. 1 Brindleyplace.

Workers from Jarrett & Rainsford enjoy a staff outing to Matlock in 1906. It is recorded that the firm gave them all a free midday dinner. The original six workers from 1860 apparently earned £7 0s 10d per week, working a ten-hour day, six days a week.

An 1872 advertisement for G.E. Belliss & Co., the well-known steam compressors and boilermakers. At this time the address was Broad Street, Islington: Islington was the name given to the street from Oozells Street to Five Ways. Eventually the buildings were renumbered consecutively along the whole street. Belliss linked up with Alfred Morcom who was particularly associated with the Royal Dockyards and developed steam turbines and engines. Just like the steam his company expanded, and moved into larger premises in nearby Ladywood, becoming Belliss & Morcom, a major employer.

Broad Street on a postcard, *c.* 1948. The Christian Science church dominates the left-hand side of the street looking towards the city centre. The spire is that of the Church of the Messiah. The derelict land on the left was eventually to become the site of Bush House, the city's Housing Department. The bus stop is outside Osler's glass showroom. The public house, the Granville, is now O'Neills. The pub and the large church are the only survivors today.

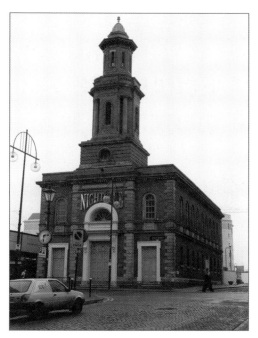

A chapel was built for the Presbyterians in 1834, and replaced by this building in 1848. It was built without any external windows, being lighted from the roof. It became a Christian Science church in 1929 and later added a reading room and Sunday school. The church survived calls for it to be demolished because of the financial burden of repairing and maintaining it. An article written in 1923 described the church as 'a complete abortion' and a 'lamentable example of the building of a church in that most unlovely of building material – blue brick'. In a controversial move the church became a nightclub, with the imaginative name The Church.

The famous 'skeleton of Broad Street', April 1956. In 1937 work began to construct a building as a training centre for Odeon cinemas, but the Second World War meant work couldn't progress and the structure was left to be occasionally wire-brushed and painted. It was rumoured that Woolworth's would take over the building after 1945 but in 1956, when work recommenced, it became the city's Housing Department headquarters. The large white building is the A1 Tyre Company.

Bush House opened on the corner of Cumberland Street on 27 March 1958; it was the largest city council housing department building in Europe. The 657 staff moved out in 1989 and demolition took place in December 1990. Cumberland Street was also home to Mitchell's pen works and Barbarella's nightclub.

Bush House, August 1989. The small white building was the Five Ways Working Men's Club. It was the first building to be built way back from the street edge to enable subsequent road widening to take place; this never happened. Next to it the French-owned Novotel was being built.

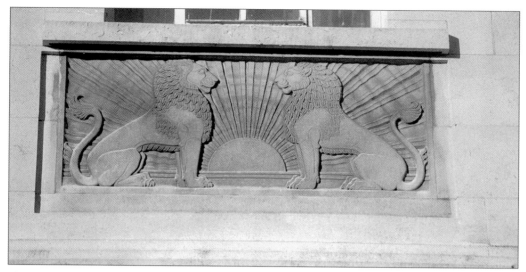

The Five Ways Working Men's Club was a victim of the changing face of Broad Street. It was established in 1906 and the British lion and the rising sun were depicted in the stonework: this was said to be 'symbolic of the dawn of a new era for working men'. In 1925 it had 800 members but numbers dwindled and it closed in 1938 because 'the tentacles of the city have spread even further afield, removing the working-class population from the central areas to rehousing districts in the outskirts'.

The Patent Metallic Air Tight Coffin Company occupied one of the buildings that was formerly on the site of Bush House. Coffins were 'air tight and water tight so no injurious or offensive effluvia' could escape. Turkish baths and a servants' home were also located there. According to the 1881 census 41 per cent of females aged sixteen to twenty were 'in service'.

Oozells Street, showing part of the Oozells Street Board School and the former foundry of H. Piercy & Co. The manager of the machine shop lived above the foundry. It has been suggested that the name Oozells derives from Ousel Cocks (or blackbirds), which once sang in the hedgerows in the fields here. Others suggest Oozells may have meant 'high houses', Lozells meaning 'low houses', or that the area once belonged to a man called Odingsell, of which Oozells is a corruption.

The forlorn derelict former Oozells Street Board School as it looked in about 1987. It was built to the design of Martin and Chamberlain in 1877 and when it opened on 28 January 1878 there were 807 primary school age children. In later years it became a college and a furniture store for the education department.

The future of the Oozells Street Board School building was uncertain and demolition seemed a likely option. It was rescued at the final hour after demolition contracts had been drawn up. The interior of the building was a burned-out wreck. This is how it looked in July 1995. Following the awarding of numerous grants the building reopened in March 1998 as the Ikon Gallery.

The former caretaker's house at the rear of the building. It may originally have been the headmaster's house. Sadly this was demolished to make way for the Water's Edge development at Brindleyplace. In the background stands the soon to be completed NIA.

A new tower completed the Ikon building. The original tower was demolished on safety grounds in 1976. The photo on p. 54 shows the flat roof, partly hidden by the tree, where the tower once stood. Painstaking research resulted in the tower being built as accurately as possible to the original design. Here the author of this book takes a close look at the progress of the tower in April 1997.

This block of houses on nearby Sheepcote Street, awaiting demolition, was typical of the dwellings in the catchment area of Oozells Street School. When wholesale slum clearance began pupil numbers dwindled, and this was no doubt a factor in the decision to close the school and reopen it in 1898 as a specialist secondary school, the George Dixon Higher Grade School, specialising in science-related subjects. Ironically Sheepcote Street is now one of the most popular areas for upmarket residential properties, and a number of old warehouses and factories have been converted into apartments.

BIRMINGHAM LABOUR CHURCH
CINDERELLA CLUB.

Xmas Treat to Slum Children.

WE propose to feed **2,000** of the very poorest and most neglected bairns this Xmas, and we appeal, once more, with confidence, for help which has never been refused us at this Season of the year, to obtain the means to feed such a multitude of little ones. We need

200 Plum Puddings. **2,000** Apples or Oranges.
2,000 Mince Pies.   **3 cwt.** of Sweets.

A Xmas Tree will be given to **350** additional very young mites, and we appeal for TOYS to decorate the same.

PLUM PUDDINGS and MINCE PIES may be sent, **not later** than December 28th, to Hon. Secretary.—

A. LL. MATTHISON,
320, SUMMER LANE.

RONALD L. SPEARS, Hon. Assist. Secy.,
48, GODWIN STREET, BLOOMSBURY,

or to one of the following Committee:—

MRS. SAYERS,   A. GRIFFIN,   G. B. KING,
W. POWELL and P. M. STURGE.

For a short while the Oozells Street Board School building was home to the Birmingham Labour Church, which helped poor local youngsters through its Cinderella Club. This poster was produced for their Christmas appeal in 1898. The children were taken on outings to Sutton Park.

ESTABLISHED 1860.

WILLIAM GRIMES,
Coal Merchant,
OOZELLS-ST. WHARF, BROAD STREET
BIRMINGHAM.

PRESENT PRICES.

Deep Coal	...	...	19s.6d. per ton	Kibbles ...	14s.6d. to 15s.6d. per ton
„ Lumps	...	...	18s. „ „	Rongh Slack ...	10s.6d. to 13s.6d. „
Cobbles	...	...	16s.6d. „ „	Fine Slack ...	7s.6d. „

One-Way, (a first class Coal for domestic purposes,) 18s. per ton.

NO CHARGE FOR DELIVERY.

2½ per cent. discount allowed on orders of 5 tons and upwards for cash on delivery

Special Quotations to large consumers.

Manufacturers supplied with all kinds of Coal and Slack by boat on any Canal.

Orders are respectfully solicited and may be addressed to 122, ALSTON-ST., LADYWOOD

The canal network included a loop along which numerous wharves were built to enable coal to be unloaded and finished goods removed from nearby factories. This advertisement appeared in *The Edgbaston and Ladywood Advertiser and Literary Repository*. In 1879 William Grimes was one of thirteen coal merchants at the wharf.

This is the Oozells Street loop canal wharf in September 1986. The street was cut from Broad Street to the canal in 1837–8. Oozells Street North backs on to it from the left. Today the Brindleyplace car park occupies most of the wharf area.

From this large Modern Factory...

. . . Covering over 800,000 square feet of floor space, and provided with all amenities for the workers, including Canteen, Rest-room, Roof Games-Courts, etc., and equipped with the latest High-speed Precision Machinery in the Wood, Metal and Bedding Departments, etc., come some of the Finest Products in the Trade. Over 50 years' experience has built up and maintains an unbroken reputation for Quality, Value and Service.

BUYERS ARE INVITED TO SEE OUR FINE SHOWROOMS. to go through our WORKS, and to inspect our Timber Wharf. **A visit is both interesting and profitable!**

WOOD COTS
CHILDREN'S BEDS
NURSERY FURNITURE
PLAYPENS, ETC.

ESTABLISHED OVER 50 YEARS

WOOD BEDS
IRON BEDSTEADS
MATTRESSES, DIVANS
BEDDING, ETC.

The Atlas Works on Oozells Street was a major employer in the area. The company made wire mattresses and metal bedsteads. In later years the premises became well known as Birmingham's car tax centre.

Jack Powell, on the left, was the son of the founder of the Atlas Works. He is pictured with the author of this book as he tells a group of local people about the history of the factory, which can be seen on the photograph that is being held up. That view shows a 1986 perspective of the derelict factory as it awaits demolition to make way for the National Sea Life Centre. Jack unveiled a street sign for Atlas Way, which was the name given to the walkway between the National Sea Life Centre and the canal.

This May 1986 view shows the remaining factories, which once thrived on the canal side adjacent to the canal island. It is not really an island at all, but more of a safety device, erected during the Second World War. The plan was that if an enemy bomb breached a branch of the canal then shutters could be put across from the island to the towpath, so the amount of water loss would be minimised and the canal network would still be operational. The major railway line to the city centre from the north-west runs beneath the canal on the left.

The same view as above but twelve years later, when Birmingham was hosting the World Leaders G8 Summit and the canals were packed with delegates, journalists and tourists. Immediately on the left stands the Malthouse pub, built on the site of a former malthouse. The largest building is the Energy Centre, which provides power for the ICC and NIA. The junction is called Old Turn Junction, and a signpost on the island indicates that Wolverhampton is 13 miles and 3 locks away, Fazeley 15 miles and 38 locks and Worcester 30 miles and 58 locks.

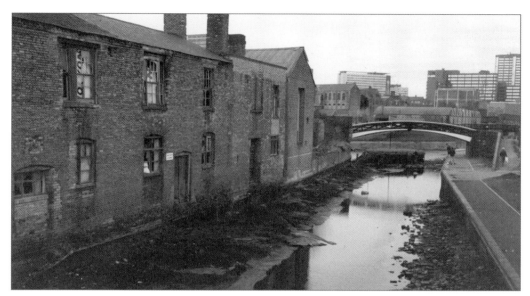

A derelict scene after the canal was drained for cleaning and repairs. The building, known as Kingston Wharf, is a rare surviving example of Victorian canalside architecture with doorways opening on to the canal at barge level. It was erected in about 1790 as a nail and iron warehouse. The original proprietors were Theodore and Philemon Price. Philemon lived in the Crescent. The building fell into disrepair and became a blot on the landscape before being converted into an engineering centre.

Kingston Wharf in November 1993 with one of the early tourist boats. Edward Heath launched *Europe* in 1975 to commemorate Great Britain's entry into the EEC.

The Crescent Theatre on Cumberland Street opened in 1964 and this is how it looked in 1990. It has now been replaced by an office block.

The theatre found itself in the spotlight when plans for Brindleyplace were unveiled, because the street was to disappear for an office development. It exited stage left to a new site a few minutes' walk away. Chairman Ron Barber led the celebrations to mark the turnover of the first sod from the new site on Sheepcote Street.

An artist's impression of The Water's Edge looking onto The International Convention Centre

An artist's impression of the Water's Edge development at Brindleyplace opposite the canalside entrance of the ICC. This was a publicity postcard published to advertise that building work had started in September 1993. The reverse side says, 'It certainly looks the best opportunity around for retailers and restaurateurs today'. It adds there are lots of places to stay nearby and key developers have already signed up for an opening in July 1994.

Over two million people visit the Water's Edge each year, spending nearly £14 million. In October 1995 the development won the prestigious 'Excellence on the Waterfront Award', which had previously been won by Sydney, Tokyo, Toronto and Amsterdam. This scene is from the 2001 Inland Waterways Festival, which was centred on the canal network from the Water's Edge to Cambrian Wharf.

The topping out ceremony at the BT offices at no. 5 Brindleyplace, 29 May 1996. Topping out is a traditional builders' ceremony which marks the completion of the main structure of a building. A twig of yew was placed on the highest part of the building to ward off evil spirits. The BT building is one of the most impressive of the new buildings at Brindleyplace.

The most impressive of the office blocks on Brindleyplace is the imaginatively titled 'no. 3 Brindleyplace'. It is home to Grimley, Royal Mail and Regus. It includes a colonnade entrance and magnificent central atrium. There is a 180 feet high clock tower, which dominates the skyline as the old brewery towers once did from across the canal at the Crown Brewery. Once completed Brindleyplace Square will be home to nearly 10,000 office workers. Each building has been erected in a different style, giving a timeless feel to the area.

At the launch of an education pack about Brindleyplace in December 1995 children from local schools unveiled a 20 ft high bronze sculpture called The Aqueduct. (Yes, I know there is no real aqueduct anywhere near Brindleyplace!) Alan Chatham, director of Brindleyplace, and Norman Bartlam, who co-wrote the pack, can be seen between the main parts of the sculpture looking somewhat startled, as extremely loud fireworks were set off when the drape was pulled down!

The sculpture can be seen in the lower left of this view of Brindleyplace Square. The fountain forms a centrepiece to the square and 88,000 gallons of water per hour flow through it. The spaceship-shaped building is the NIA. In front of it is the ray-shaped National Sea Life Centre.

The tunnel in the shark tank is lowered into position at the National Sea Life Centre. This is the country's first 360-degree tunnel: you can see sharks swimming beneath you. The centre holds 385,000 gallons of water, 330,000 of which arrived at the centre in a fleet of tankers after being collected in the sea off Weymouth beach.

Two pupils from Summerfield Junior School, Nelson Rahi and Radha Rani, help staff unload the fish at the centre in June 1996.

The National Sea Life Centre was officially opened, underwater, by Olympic swimmer Sharron Davies and her athlete husband Phil Redmond, on 2 July 1996.

The site of the NIA, September 1986. The main railway between Birmingham and the north-west goes through the middle of a natural basin. Planners regarded this amphitheatre as 'one of those obstructions to a proper growth of the city'. A plan had been drawn up to put a road on stilts over the basin through the area to Ladywood to 'effectively open up the area and pleasure seekers would be given a suitable and direct approach to a proposed recreation ground', which was to be built in Ladywood. Eventually the site was chosen for a coach and car park for the ICC, but this plan was also altered, and eventually the scrap metal merchants' yards and railway sidings were removed for the £50 million arena.

This view of June 1989 shows Stephenson's railway arch, which was built between 1846 and 1847 to take the railway underground into the city centre. The two tall office blocks are on Broad Street, and between them stand the derelict Oozells Street Board School and the blue brick Christian Science Church. Bush House stands on the extreme right.

The railway was bridged over, extending the tunnel to the St Vincent Street Bridge, and the main indoor arena was built on top of it. This view was taken in August 1989. Linford Christie opened the Arena in October 1991. It has a six-lane, 200-metre demountable running track.

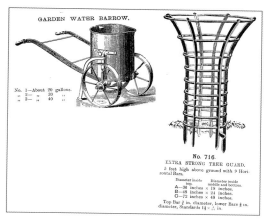

GARDEN WATER BARROW.

No. 1—About 20 gallons.
 „ 2— „   30
 „ 3— „   40

No. 716.
EXTRA STRONG TREE GUARD.
5 feet high above ground with 9 Horizontal Bars.

Diameter inside top.   Diameter inside middle and bottom.
A—36 inches × 18 inches.
B—48 inches × 24 inches.
C—72 inches × 48 inches.
Top Bar ⅞ in. diameter, lower Bars ⅝ in. diameter, Standards 1¼ × ⅜ in.

THE
"QUADRANT" TRICYCLE
NO. 9.

(SIDE STEERING.)

Same as No. 8, but open fronted, with adjustable spade handle on either side, the right hand steering and the left operating the brake. A most elegant Tricycle, suitable for either gentleman or lady.

Price same as No. 8.   Dress guard, 7 6 extra.

Sheepcote Street was a street of many manufacturing trades: Stewart & Lloyd's tubes, Baxter's screws and Hudson Edmund's brass tube works were the largest employers but many smaller firms existed. Ewell's made extra strong tree guards and garden water barrows, the Patent Ferrule Company manufactured Shoebotham's signal balls and Quadrant bicycles was one of 450 bicycle manufacturers in Birmingham in 1900.

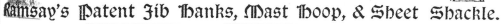

THE PATENT FERRULE CO.,

MANUFACTURERS OF PATENT

SHIPS THIMBLES

SHOEBOTHAM'S PATENT "COLLAPSE" SIGNAL BALLS.

Ramsay's Patent Jib Hanks, Mast Hoop, & Sheet Shackle.

OLVER'S PATENT TOGGLE,

IMPROVED SOLID FORGED SPECTACLE CLEWS,

ALL KINDS OF SHIPPING TACKLE,

MALLEABLE AND WROUGHT IRON HINGES,

For Ship Builders' Sail Makers' and Riggers' Purposes.

Patent Converted Steel and Iron Ferrules

For Locomotive, Marine, and other Tubular Boilers, also for Agricultural Engineers, Wood Turners, and Edge Tool Makers.

STAMPED FORGINGS AND GENERAL SMITH'S WORK.

SHEEPCOTE STREET, BIRMINGHAM.

LONDON OFFICES.
WITTY and WYATT, 9, Fenchurch Street, London.

Sykes' woodworking business was established on Sheepcote Street in 1862. It backed on to the scrapyard where the NIA was later to be built. This view of the timber yard was taken in 1898.

At the bottom of Sheepcote Street stands a horseshoe-shaped stables popularly called the Roundhouse. It was formerly the mineral and coal wharf belonging to the Midland & North-Western Railway Company and the wharf manager lived in one of the gatehouses. This was how it appeared before extensive renovation was carried out to turn it into a popular pub and craft centre: six of the original stables still exist. The pub building was once a school.

4

The West End &
Five Ways

The hexagonal paving of Five Ways Island is prominent in this view from September 1973. New development is under way along Hagley Road, and the derelict land is the site of Tesco. Broad Street runs off to the right.

This view from November 1954 shows, above ground-floor level, a range of architectural styles. The Richard Motors building dates from around 1879 when it was a surgeon's house. The Williams family were drysalters and oil merchants from at least 1888. The building on the right was a car showroom with a dance studio above.

Broad Street at the junction of Sheepcote Street on a postcard of *c*. 1902. The impressive corner building was a bank. It was spared demolition during the 1990s redevelopment and is now a restaurant appropriately named Left Bank. It bears a datestone of 1836, although it probably became the Birmingham District Counties Bank in 1898. On the other side of the street carcasses of meat can be seen hanging outside Tyler's butcher's shop.

The corner of Sheepcote Street, showing the bank and hospital, November 1964. The hospital building dates from around 1815 when it was the residence of Mr Rice, a local glass manufacturer. The hospital was founded as the Children's Hospital in 1861. It was seen as 'a means of alleviating the suffering of those blossoms of Humanity who, without its tender aid, might in the budding of life, have faded out of existence altogether'.

The hospital, c. 1880. The stone column on the corner wall, built in about 1860, still stands. It bears a faded inscription, which probably reads: 'This stone records the building of this wall and railings to the sole cost of two farthings.'

REGINALD WILSON

"They Aint Arf Good at the 'Cripples'"

For many years the hospital was known as the Royal Orthopaedic Hospital, or more affectionately as 'The Cripples'. This sketch appeared in a 1938 magazine advertising a fund-raising event for the hospital. The hospital building closed in March 1994, and pints of blood have been exchanged for pints of beer, as it is now the Old Orleans pub and restaurant.

Looking from the hospital towards Five Ways, January 1953. The small building to the left of the tree was the Dolls' Hospital where broken dolls were repaired. One of the shops was rumoured to be the place where the ropes were purchased to enable one of the so-called Great Train Robbers to escape from Winson Green prison.

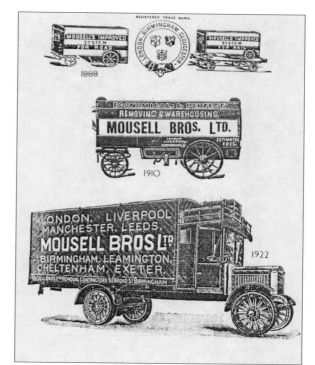

Mousell's removals were on this site from at least 1878 until the late 1960s. In 1878 they advertised themselves as 'The largest in the world'. A 1910 advert promised 'experience, efficiency and economy'. These adverts, which show a range of styles, from 1888 to 1922, illustrate how Mousell's removals moved with the times!

Ryland Place and Ryland Street. This was once a thriving shopping parade serving commuters and residents of Ladywood who lived in the streets behind Broad Street. Ryland was a wealthy landowner who laid out this area of Broad Street. The photograph was taken in September 1953: the cars at West Midland Motors were still mainly all black, but this was the month in which Ford announced two new car models for Britain, the Anglia and the Prefect, which would be available in bright colours.

Astley's costumiers and theatrical shop was on the corner of Ruston Street from the late 1890s until demolition in the late 1960s. The pub on the left is the Victoria Inn. The street is named in honour of Martha Ruston, the maiden name of Mrs Ryland.

In 1976 office blocks and Tesco opened on the site of these shops between Ruston Street and Five Ways. It was originally planned as the West End entertainment area, with a 1,100-seat cinema and 80-bed hotel. Ironically a cinema complex was built over the road thirty years later. This view shows 126–35 Broad Street in February 1964. Dawson ironmongers, Wilton's clothes shop and Hurrell's provision stores were long-established traders. Vicker's was a baker's. Just off the picture were Barrow's, Skinner's shoe shop and Crowe's tobacconists.

Ordered, that the following Gentlemen ... be added to the Trustees which were appointed by order Dated the 30th April 1788 for forming and gravelling the Road from Bridge Street in Birmingham to the five Ways Turnpike ...

Ordered that a Turnpike House & two Turnpike Gates with proper Posts & Rails be forthwith erected & set up at a certain Place upon the said Road near the Town of Birmingham called the Five Ways

2/7/1773

Text from the official records of the turnpike trust shows that a decision to build a tollgate at Five Ways was taken in July 1773. The trustees were authorised to 'borrow any sum of money not exceeding £800'. It is recorded in 1796 that an order was given 'that the road between Five Ways and Birmingham be occasionally scraped during the winter and the dirt carried off as soon as possible'. The following year an additional order was signed for 'strong gravel' at 'under the price of one shilling per load of 30 cwt, 200 loads to be immediately purchased and laid upon the road between Birmingham and the Five Ways Gate where it may be wanted and that the gravel now lying upon the sides of the road be spread there on'. The second extract for gravelling the road is dated 30 April 1798.

A sketch of the tollgate that stood from 1773 to July 1841 at Five Ways. Benjamin Burbridge was chosen as the collector of tolls, and it is recorded that he 'shall receive for his trouble there seven shillings a week'; by 1774 he was earning 9s a week. In 1789 the keeper was ordered 'not to sell bread or any other article at the said gate'. Two hundred years later Tesco moved in.

Five Ways on a postcard used in April 1905. The Georgian House in the centre of the picture still stands today. The statue and clock are also still at Five Ways, although they have been re-sited. Calthorpe Road goes off to the left and Hagley Road to the right. The turreted building was the Midland Bank, which stood at the corner of Ladywood Road.

A policeman on traffic control duty, 1947. Traffic was to become even more of a problem in later years, leading to the Five Ways island development which almost completely changed the area. The building with a triangular roof behind the bus in the distance is the one pictured on the postcard above. It survived demolition and still stands today.

An undated postcard of Five Ways. Notice the aerial tram wires. In 1904 Lee Longland's successfully petitioned against trams being routed along Broad Street. Mr Longland apparently thought they would lower the tone of the street, which was regarded as 'the gateway to Edgbaston'. Consequently trams travelled from the city via Holloway Head, across Five Ways and on to Ladywood Road.

Five Ways, 1997. The building on the left is the Georgian House, which appears on the earlier postcard views. The flags are flying from the roof of the Swallow Hotel, which was erected in 1958 as the headquarters of the Tube Investments Company. It was built on a tree-lined park, which can be seen behind the statue in the view above this one. When erected it was said to be 'a vista on the approach from the civic centre which will justify the description as The Gateway to Edgbaston'.

Five Ways, looking out of the city along Hagley Road, December 1960. The building on the right is the King Edward VI Grammar School, which opened on this site in 1883. In 1958 the school moved to the Birmingham suburb of Bartley Green. A plaque on the ground in the Five Ways island indicates where the school building once stood. Notice the police call box on the island.

The statue of Joseph Sturge at Five Ways. The written message on this postcard reads: 'Ted, Rudolph and I came up by bus at 9.15 and have seen the university, Town Hall, Cathedral and St Martin's Church and the Burne Jones windows. It was quite a job to drag R. from some of the shops. Of course all the natives were interested. We went first to two or three shops but found that size 11 tennis shoes are not stocked! We are at present having dinner in the Cobden Café. R. doesn't drink tea and Ted is drinking lemonade – while I've got a whole tea service to play about with for 3d.' A PS adds 'Five Ways K.E. Grammar School in right background'.

Joseph Sturge (1793–1859) was a pacifist and campaigner against slavery. He also founded an Adult School; the last Sunday of his life was spent at nearby Severn Street School where he worked 'to bring together in the body of Christ the working class and well to do'. The statue is flanked by female figures representing Peace and Charity. The unveiling of the statue in 1862 was attended by 12,000 people. Joseph Sturge travelled to the West Indies to campaign for the emancipation of the slaves, setting up a plantation to prove that it could be run profitably without slave labour. On his return in 1837 over 500 people attended a breakfast given 'for the purpose of congratulating him on his safe return and to express the sense of his unwearied and philanthropic exertions in the cause of Negro emancipation'. In later years a member of his family set up a lime and sugar plantation, the products of which proved extremely useful in the battle against alcoholism. The Temperance Society report of 1891 reads: 'Our principles now permeate all classes: and the work of this, which began 60 years ago, and was thought to be the feeble outburst of fanaticism, has become an acknowledged powerful agency in raising the people to the position an intelligent community ought to occupy.'

A view of Five Ways from Hagley Road looking towards Broad Street, as it appeared on a postcard franked November 1906. The clock indicates the time was 4.20 p.m., but it seems unlikely the passengers on the horse-drawn bus will have left their place of work or finished their city centre shopping early to avoid the traffic congestion that was to occur at Five Ways! The words 'bottleneck' and 'rush hour' do not seem to have been invented, although the boys by the handcart may well be saying something derogatory about the speed of the bus which was heading towards Bearwood!

Lloyds Bank on the corner of Islington Row. The first suburban branch of Lloyds Bank opened near here in 1874 and moved to this site in 1882. The building was rebuilt in Portland stone in 1908.

Lloyds Bank can be seen behind the trees in this picturesque late 1950s scene. The parkland was eventually built on and an office block for Tube Investments, which later became a hotel, was built there. The Five Ways clock can just be seen behind the bus.

Five Ways then and now. This postcard was franked September 1912. The correspondent wrote 'You will recognize this view'. Would they recognise the same view nearly seventy years later, as it looks on the lower picture? The only common feature is the Lloyds Bank building on the right. The building behind the clock was home to a branch of the Birmingham Dairy Co. and later the National Provincial Bank. Next door stood Hewitt's flower shop and Chase's chemist.

Taken from the same viewpoint, March 1981. The scene is now dominated by the Auchinleck Square office block with its colourful façade. This photograph was taken from the front of the Georgian building. The clock has been re-sited just to the left of the photograph.

Five Ways, looking towards Hagley Road from the junction of Islington Row and Broad Street, on a postcard franked 1926. The trams made tracks along Islington Row past the front of the clock and on to Ladywood Road. The lone bicyclist carefully guides his bicycle between the rails, eager not to become entangled! The clock states it is eight o'clock and already a few eager schoolboys are perhaps on their way to King Edward's Five Ways School, which is the turreted building behind Sturge's statue. The block lettering on the buildings on the right reads 'Five Ways Fish Hall'.

The Fish Hall is on the left of this view looking towards Islington Row and Broad Street. A tram is heading for the city centre via Islington Row, while the motorbus advertising Sames pianos and Schweppes drinks is coming up Broad Street. The canopies are down shielding the shop window displays from the sun.

The Five Ways clock was erected in honour of the first coroner of the Borough, John Birt Davies, who held office for thirty-six years. During that time he reportedly sat through 30,000 inquests, never took a holiday or appointed a deputy and never spent a night outside the borough. He died in December 1878 at the age of seventy-nine and the clock is a tribute to him.

The Five Ways clock was an invaluable timepiece as very few people had watches and even factory timekeepers kept an eye on it. In 1936 workers at Kunzle's, the building in the centre of this 1950s photograph, complained that '"his" time keeping ways are indeed whimsical and show a complete lack of self-control. We are beginning to feel desperate about the situation.' The men in charge of the clock ticked Kunzle's off, stating that 'the clock is checked every week and the utmost variation would not exceed 10–15 seconds per week'.

Work under way to complete the Five Ways traffic island and underpass, 1970. This junction had become a notorious bottleneck and thirty years later the problem has returned! The junction was completed in record time, less than twelve months, faster than any other similar traffic system in the Midlands. This is the underpass, which takes traffic from Hagley Road under the island into Broad Street. When completed it was discovered that the headroom under part of the tunnel was 16 ft 5¾ in, a quarter of an inch below the regulation 16 ft 6 in, so part of the road surface was shaved off to meet the stringent rules! The office block is part of the new Auchinleck Square shopping centre.

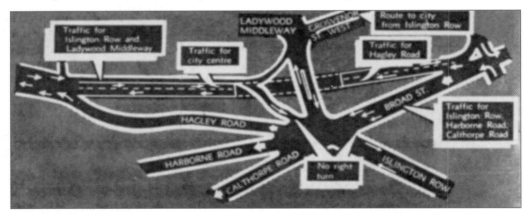

During construction of the Five Ways island there was a complicated road pattern for motorists to negotiate. This map was produced to help confused drivers. At first only one carriageway was open to traffic. The official advice was: 'Traffic going into the city, along the Hagley Road, should use the off-side lane for Broad Street, going via the underpass, and the near-side for Islington Row, when it will use the surface level roads, crossing over the underpass. These lane directions are the opposite to those which are in use now.' It added: 'Traffic for Broad Street from Islington Row will be directed via Ladywood Middleway, Grosvenor Street and Ryland Street.' They could have added: 'Confused? Then why not catch a bus and be on the first buses ever to use an underpass in Birmingham.'

This aerial view shows that it could be argued that six roads meet at Five Ways! The largest building at the junction is Lloyds Bank. Across the road note King Edward's School, which stretches back from Hagley Road. Broad Street runs off to the top of the photograph, which probably dates from the early 1950s.

This September 1973 view shows the completed 'gyratory traffic system' and shopping centre. The road improvement scheme was opened in 1971. The land on the left had been cleared to make way for the Broadway office development and Tesco. Broad Street disappears into the distance.

This postcard franked 1907 shows on the right the decorating firm of John Taylor and Chase's chemist shop. Taylor proudly boasted of winning prizes and medals for his work at international events in London and Paris. His father was a career soldier and enlisted at the age of twelve. He was said at one time to have been 'the only living man in England who could have been concerned in any battles of the eighteenth century'.

Another view of Broad Street decked out for the royal visit in 1909. The Five Ways Inn is on the immediate left of this view looking towards the Waterworks Arch. At this end of the street the crowd was enlivened by the appearance of Colonel Ludlow's detachment of Territorials marching from Ladywood Road police station, headed by a goat, the regimental mascot.

Horse-drawn buses have been replaced by motorbuses in this view. Alderman Bowater, a former Lord Mayor and Broad Street resident, once recalled: 'the fare on this bus was four pence inside and three pence outside. Those fares represented the minimum charges, however short the distance travelled. In inclement weather the inside passengers remained dry and the outside passengers did not. Personally I could never understand why, in sunny weather, the rates were not reversed for the interior was so cramped and pokey in the summer that there was always danger of asphyxiation.' He added: 'At Five Ways the conductor would disappear into the inn, and reappear a few moments later with a jug of beer, which the driver drank with evident enjoyment and much smacking of the lips. This ceremony was observed on every single journey.'

Traffic is increasing and it has been found necessary to have a policeman on traffic duty. A Broad Street-based photographer called Moules produced this postcard in 1932.

The Kunzle building as it looked in 1937. Christian Kunzle (1879–1954) set up the factory. The company newspaper, the *Kunzle Gazette*, reported: 'In 1910 the factory consisted of a bake house, chocolate covering and starch rooms and a packing office. There were about fifty employees. The firm had one van and a horse for delivery purposes. Towards the end of 1911 things began to move rather quickly. Kunzle was a name just beginning to be talked about, and much excitement was caused when the first wholesale turnover reached £28 in one week. The business moved to Garrett's Green in about 1964.'

Kunzle owned a chateau in Davos in Switzerland, and in May 1932 he sent a group of his employees who suffered from bronchitis, asthma or tuberculosis, for a three-month visit. After that he sent children from the local area on visits. He hoped the dry pure air and Swiss cream and milk would help alleviate their symptoms. Pete Judd who is pictured on p. 92 is seen here at Snow Hill station, awaiting a train to start the trip to the home of the man who had a chateau with a gateau. The taller of the two men on the right is Christian Kunzle.

A double-decker bus travels out of the city centre along Broad Street past the largest building in the photograph, Kunzle's chocolate and cake manufactory. Travelling along Broad Street was still a piece of cake in those days compared to the congestion that built up within a few years. The road to the right is Islington Row. The National Provincial Bank stands on the corner and on the opposite side of Broad Street is the Five Ways Inn.

A page from Kunzle's works magazine in 1935, which depicts the feverish activity in the build-up to Christmas.

In March 2000 a plaque was erected by the Civic Society at Five Ways shopping centre to commemorate the site of the Kunzle factory. By remarkable coincidence the man who erected the plaque was Pete Judd, the little lad pictured on p. 90 who benefited from a trip to Switzerland.

This is Auchinleck House at Five Ways shopping centre as it nears completion in July 1964. Many of the shopkeepers who were displaced by redevelopment moved into the new centre. The block is called Auchinleck House after Field Marshal Sir Claude Auchinleck (1884–1981) who was the Commander of the Armed Forces in India and the Middle East at various stages of his career. His claim to fame on Broad Street was that he became chairman of the company that built the block.

This July 1957 view illustrates superbly the range of everyday shops that occupied this site. The occupants included Wimbush, bakers, Wrenson's, grocers, and Boots the chemist. Further up stood the long-established premises of Crowe, Wilton's clothes, Hedge's the chemist, Gough's the butcher and Seer's the decorator, to name just a few. This photo was taken in the week that Stirling Moss won the British Grand Prix, prompting many a police officer to stop speeding motorists with the line 'Excuse me sir, who do you think you are, Stirling Moss?'

Today this is the site of new food outlets and bars, but things were much gentler in July 1950, the time of this scene. It was a nice line of convenience stores, which led up to the corner of St Martin's Street. The tall building was a post office, later to become a servicemen's club and then a nightclub. The other shops included Poole's grocers, Harris' cleaners, Christine's outfitters and the Britannia Building Society. This was the month in which the government announced the ending of soap rationing.

F. WILTON,

Cloakmaker, Manufacturing

Furrier,

LADIES' OUTFITTER, ETC.,
FRENCH MANTLES, . .
HIGH-CLASS JACKETS, . .
COATS AND PALETÒTS. .

Tailor-Made Gowns.

THE LATEST MODES

In Millinery, Rich Sealskin, Caracul,
and Broad Tail Coats, Russian and
Canadian Sables, Chinchillas, Min-
ever, Ermine, Astrachan, and all
fashionable Furs.

Sealskins remodelled by Experienced Furriers on the premises.

*Funerals Conducted and arrangements made in all
parts of the country.*

FIVE WAYS HOUSE,

139, 140 & 141, BROAD STREET, BIRMINGHAM.

Proof if ever it were needed that this end of
Broad Street catered for every need. Wilton's was
one of the longest established businesses, closing
in the early 1990s; the advert dates from 1902.
The chilblains advert is from 1882, and the
shoeing one from 1876. Tennant Street ran
behind Broad Street.

CHILBLAINS

AGARICUS MUSCARIUS
LINIMENT.

This Liniment has been used many
years; its largely-increased sale
has proved its efficacy in this very
distressing complaint.
    The parts affected to be rubbed
with a brush (attached to the cork)
as frequently as convenient.

**In Bottles, 1s., 1s.6d., and
2s. 6d. each.**

    If the Chilblains are broken,
Calendula Cerate is used
which has very healing properties.
*A little to be spread on a bit of Lint,
and applied twice a day.*

In Pots, 1s., and 2s. each.

Prepared especially by

EDWARD CORFIELD,

Homœopathic Dispensing Chemist,

166, BROAD STREET,

BIRMINGHAM.

Associate of the Pharmaceutical
Society of Great Britain.

ESTABLISHED 1860.

THE ORIGINAL

SHOEING FORGE

AND

General Jobbing Smith,

144, TENNANT STREET,

BIRMINGHAM.

T. ANDREWS,

PROPRIETOR.

T.A. begs to return his sincere thanks to his
numerous customers and patrons for their liberal
support during the sixteen years he has been in
business, and hopes, by strict attention to all
orders entrusted to his care, to merit a contin-
uance of their special favours.

A view of Curry's electrical store, which stood at the corner of Bishopsgate Street, January 1964. This was erected as a temporary structure in 1909! Next door stood a branch of the Co-op. Just prior to demolition a restaurant there was called Regards to Broad Street. The youths who bought their record players at this time would have bopped along to the number one hits 'Glad All Over' and 'Needles and Pins'.

The same site today showing the recently opened multi-screen UGC complex which has attracted large numbers of people to this end of Broad Street.

Right Hon. the Lord Mayor of Birmingham,
Alderman W. H. Bowater. J.P.

A view from the corner of Bishopsgate Street in January 1964, showing the premises of Skefko ball bearings, Stanford & Mann, the well-known stationers and the Immanuel Parish Church and chapel. In the 1860s this was home to the Magdalen Asylum and Free Registry for Destitute Girls, which was 'A penitentiary to reclaim from a life of sin those unfortunate females who profess themselves desirous to return to the paths of virtue and happiness'. Those desirous of happiness today can visit the Hard Rock Café and nearby casino which opened on the site in October 2001.

No. 207 Broad Street, now the site of Brannigan's bar, was the workplace of William Bowater, a dentist who in 1878 'respectfully called attention to the superiority of his newly-invented Rugosite suction palate'. It 'defied all competition for natural appearance, mastication, comfort, and durability'. He got his teeth stuck into politics and became Lord Mayor of Birmingham. He was knighted in 1916 for his war work: he recruited, raised and helped to equip the Birmingham battalions. Later he became Deputy Lord Lieutenant of Warwickshire.

Hangers, P.J. Evans and Watson's were all car dealers at the time of this photograph in January 1964. Watson's is now Key Largo and Evans is Stoodi Bakers.

The taller building is Transport House, built for the Transport and General Workers' Union in about 1920. Next door stood Bell Barn typewriter centre. Journalists were busy that week, in May 1954, typing out the news that Roger Bannister had broken the four-minute mile.

The Dolls' Hospital, which closed shortly after this photograph was taken in 1955, was next to Spring Grove, a laundry, Salisbury's butchers and Austen J. Beeny. Beeny's, established in 1860, was said to be haunted by the ghost of a man called Tarbuck, who ran a shoe shop there at the turn of the century! Charles Albert Beeny began the Broad Street link further up the street at no. 226, near Lee Longland, before moving a few doors away to no. 217, the shop in the picture.

REPRESENTATIVES.

Who are those with anxious faces,
Seen in towns and busy places,
Journeying with weary paces,
Carrying attache cases?

Some are short and some are tall,
Some have large bags, others small,
Some are dressed in style, ye Gods !
Some are down at heel, poor ——————
But they all have anxious faces,
In the towns and busy places,
Carrying their attache cases.

Watch them and you'll see them stopping,
Into shops they keep on popping,
Then before your eyes can flicker,
Out they pop again, much quicker.

What, pray tell us, is their mission,
They that go with such precision,
Who are these poor hapless guys ?
Listen, and I'll put you wise.

These let me inform you, Sirs,
Are Commercial Travellers,
And their mission, it transpires,
Is pursuing men; called Buyers,
Who, although not blind at all,
Cannot see them when they call,
So they walk with anxious faces,
Carrying their attache cases.

Pity not their lot, my brothers,
Their reward is not as others,
When is ended their life mission,
They don't go down to perdition.

That's a fate reserved for liars,
Thieves, Sales Managers and BUYERS,
No ! their patch on earth was rough,
They were punished quite enough,
When they walked with anxious faces,
In the towns and busy places,
Journeying with weary paces,
Carrying their attache cases.

EPILOGUE.

When these poor benighted mortals,
Knock at the Celestial Portals,
Show their card and tell their story,
Open fly the Gates of Glory,
They have wiped out their transgression,
And they have a Grand Procession,
Led by Angels, playing lyres,
Last of all Ten Thousand BUYERS,
(All by forcible persuasion,
Brought from Hell for the occasion)
March behind them, several paces,
Carrying their attache cases.

Austen J. Beeny was 'a gentleman's outfitter and cotton clothing factor' when he produced this ditty about sales representatives. He called it 'A Representative's Reward. No Attaché Cases By Request!'

THE EDGBASTON & LADYWOOD ADVERTISER
& LITERARY REPOSITORY

[Established August, 1863.]   **JANUARY, 1882.**   [Entered at Stationers' Hall

BEENY'S

226, BROAD STREET

GREAT BARGAINS!

IN

Lace Curtains from 1/6 pair	Shirts from 4½d to 7/6
Blankets from 3/6 „	Stockings
Sheets from 2/9 „	Men's Cardigan and Ducks Jackets from 1/3
Quilts from 1/3 each	
Calicoes in all makes	Table Cloths
Linens from 3½d. yd.	Ladies'
Flannels from 4¾d. „	Jerseys
Blind Hollands from 6d. yard	AND Underclothing.

Often, in common with other shops, Beeny's stayed open until midnight and hung the clothes outside on hooks. The cellar was the workshop where cloth was cut to make aprons for butchers, bakers and carpenters. Charles gave way to A.J. Beeny and in 1961, when Messrs Dunn and Hand bought the name, A.J. Beeny remained on the shopfront because Beeny had such a good name in the business. They diversified and became known as the Army & Navy Stores after they began selling army surplus clothing: it was used by theatres and television companies from across the world. During the Falklands War German army boots were purchased by relations of people serving in the British army and posted to them; apparently the German boots were more suited to the conditions than the British ones! In 2000 it was swallowed up by the adjacent Bombay Mix restaurant, ending an association with Broad Street that may never be beaten.

Closing down signs dominate as proprietor Terence Hands enters his Army & Navy Stores in the last week of trading in October 2000. The name A.J. Beeny remained on the shopfront to the end. Notice that the shop lies back from the road. It is likely that originally there was a small garden in front of the shop, and the building was later extended.

A sketch showing the upmarket west end of Broad Street with the Edgbaston folk travelling home in their carriages. The spires of the Christian Science Church and the Church of the Messiah can be seen on the left.

This advertisement for one of the best-known butchers in the area dates from 1866. Ward's was next to Lee Longland's. The number 120 refers to the old street numbers, when this end of the street was called Islington.

Lloyd's perambulators, 1881.

Wharam's umbrellas were first put up in the 1870s, when the business was one of forty umbrella and parasol makers in the city. It survived until about 1940.

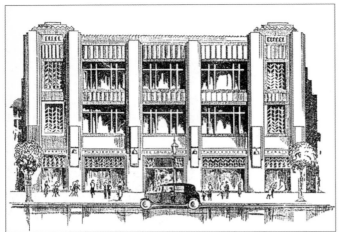

This drawing accompanied the advert for Lee Longland's when it opened here in 1931, after its removal from a site opposite the Hall of Memory. The advertising literature proudly announced: 'We look forward to welcoming our customers in surroundings which will do full justice to our stocks. The design of the building expresses the character of the inside.' The display space enabled suites to be laid out complete as they would be in people's houses – then an entirely new idea. The advert added: 'Optimists! some people will say when they hear we are moving into larger quarters – and optimists we certainly are!' That optimism was well founded, for the 1931 store expanded and is now the longest-serving on Broad Street.

Lee Longland's furniture store as it looked in March 1955. The neighbouring premises, which included Ward's was in the process of conversion into the car showroom. It has always had a slightly upmarket feel to it, appealing to the wealthier clientele who once travelled along Broad Street to their homes in the leafy suburbs. The adjacent shop, Ward's, had recently closed and H.J. Evans' cars were set to park there.

A faster form of transport replaced Lloyd's perambulators (see p. 101) by the time of this photograph, showing H.J. Evans' car showroom in November 1956. An Austin A35 was on display in the window. Lee Longland's is next door. The showroom became a nightclub called Tramps.

Osler's became very well known and opened a showroom in London. They sent out staff to India and opened up showrooms in five Indian cities supplying glass in the days of British rule. Osler had many ideas for improving the construction and design of glass chandeliers. Their works were in Freeth Street, Ladywood. A nearby secondary school, built in 1873, was named in their honour.

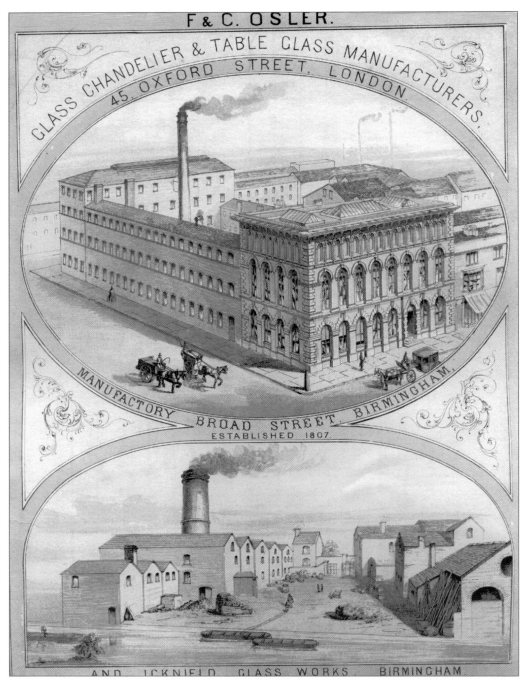

Osler's glass manufactory and showroom stood on the corner of Granville Street. In 1888 it was said in an industrial survey that the premises 'are most extensive, and consist of a substantial block of handsome appearance, used as showrooms and a long side stretch of buildings attached, which forms a manufactory. The manufactory is replete with every possible machine and appliance for the business, and a very large number of experienced hands are employed in making the world famous productions.'

Osler's designed and constructed a glass fountain that took one and a half years to produce. It was the centrepiece of the new Crystal Palace exhibition. The ruler of Egypt visited Broad Street, and was so impressed that he ordered 'a pair of candelabra of great height for the tomb of the Prophet Mahomet at Mecca'. Nothing had ever been attempted on such a grand scale before. As fashions changed Osler adapted to manufacture electric light fittings.

The Osler building, March 1955. The business transferred to Digbeth in 1960, and this magnificent building was demolished and replaced by a modern office development. The lady on the right is standing outside Lee Longland's.

The Granville pub on the corner of Granville Street. This was erected in 1923. It was once called the Westward Ho!, before returning to the Granville. Now it is an Irish theme pub, O'Neill's.

Parker, Winder & Achurch, the ironmongery concern, had the premises at the corner of Berkeley Street, and they gradually took over neighbouring buildings as they extended along the street. The smaller premises once lay back from the road and probably had small gardens in front of them. These buildings were used at various times by manufacturers of buttons, streetlights and swords. Mole's, manufacturers of swords, matchets, cutlasses, foils and pikes, was one of only two firms able to undertake government sword contracts. The other firm was Wilkinson's. One of Mole's swords is on display in the Tower of London. This 1934 photograph shows a large sign saying 'Site of new premises'. The new building is shown on the next page.

The rebuild of Parker, Winder & Achurch, 1934. This building was in turn demolished to make way for Berkeley House, home of British Telecom. The £10 million block was said to be 'an attractive feature on Broad Street'. It was topped out in 1975. Twenty years later it was converted into a hotel, now known as Jury's.

A 1935 view of the corner of Berkeley Street showing the premises of building suppliers Grosvenor Workman; later this building was taken over by Philip Fyne's, a well-known car dealer. Opposite, on the corner of Oozells Street, stands another car dealer, Reeve & Stedeford. This view also shows the Church of the Messiah, the Crown, the Prince of Wales Theatre and Bingley Hall behind it. Notice the workman attending the ornate streetlights in the central reservation; the number of cars, black cars, was increasing as the early 1930s recession eased. The bus is on route no. 1 to Acocks Green. One of the shops was popular with schoolchildren, and was known as the 'stink bomb shop'. Following demolition and rebuilding the corner became home to Allied Carpets and much later Ronnie Scott's Jazz Club.

This view of Broad Street at Gas Street corner was taken just a year before the buildings were demolished in 1964 to make way for an office block for British Rail. Beneath it was built a line of shops, which included the government bookshop and a casino. Wakefield's was a typewriter shop; next to it under the canopy was Neale's butchers. Other concerns included the Fleur de Lys restaurant and Sagger's earthenware dealers. In earlier years this was the place to go if you wanted to find the Broad Street Sick & Dividend Society or the Midland Sanitary & Decorating Company.

April 1995, and work is under way to clear the derelict factories off the corner of Gas Street and Broad Street to make way for the headquarters of Central Television. The long-established Bobby Brown's nightclub is in the distance. Fraley's stoneworks was one of the factories that was removed.

5

Around the Canals

Gas Street Basin looking towards Broad Street, 1970s. The warehouse on the left is now the site of the James Brindley pub.

Pearce & Cutler glass began as separate concerns. Solomon Cutler established a glassworks in 1854 and son Ephraim expanded into 270 Broad Street, near where Pearce established his business on Bridge Street, moving to the canalside from the city centre where he had worked since 1815. By 1920 the neighbours had amalgamated to form Pearce & Cutler in Bridge Street and they remained there until 1960. The picture shows glass arriving for Parker Winder & Achurch's new building on Broad Street in 1934.

This September 1986 view shows the chimney of the former Pearce & Cutler works from Gas Street Basin. In 1991 the factory turned into a pub called, unsurprisingly, the Glassworks. The canal went under the bridge into a private canal basin where the materials were loaded.

Sea cadets from TS *Vernon* undertake training in Gas Street Basin, 1944.

The way it was in March 1981. The block at the far end is the ATV television centre. Originally the canal continued into this area before branching off into two separate wharves, at what became known as Old Wharf.

In reflective mood on a calm Sunday, January 1987. The Pearce & Cutler chimney can be seen on the left; the buildings on the right are the newly opened offices known as The Wharf. This is a unique view made possible after land clearance. The Repertory Theatre stands out in Broad Street. Next to it are the remains of the Georgian block at the corner of King Alfred's Place and Broad Street, where the ICC now stands. The Hyatt Regency Hotel was built on the open land next to the canal bridge, rendering this view impossible today.

In September 1989 one of the last working boats, *Atlas*, was used to publicise a big canal clean-up campaign. In the background the curved wall of Symphony Hall is being constructed. In 1965 a local councillor urged the setting up of a working group to look at the economic feasibility of a hovercraft service on the canals, using the 'vast idle network of sluggish canals that lacerate the city'.

Since this photograph was taken in January 1987 a large modern cast-iron bridge, made to the 1827 design of the nearby canal bridges, has been built. Until fairly recently the only way across was via a temporary wooden structure or the plank, which on reflection was not the safest thing to do, even for cats. At that time there was no need for too many people to walk the plank; only those living and working on the narrow boats would need to use it. Today the basin has been opened to tourists and is a magnet for photographers.

Gas Street is the last resort of a retort, which was set up to extract gas from coke, hence Gas Street. John Gostling set up the business, calling it the Birmingham Light Company. He undertook to light ten streets with gaslight. Initially there were 'fearful apprehensions among the less intelligent of the population; lest the subterranean pipes of inflammable gas should in some way explode or ignite, and burn down the whole town'. Gas street lighting remained in part of the city until 1975.

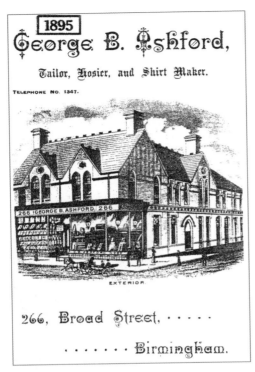

1895

George B. Ashford,

Tailor, Hosier, and Shirt Maker.

TELEPHONE NO. 1347.

EXTERIOR

266, Broad Street, ...

. . . . Birmingham.

This was the home and business premises of the tailor George Ashford. He had 'commodious quarters for the hosiery, outfitting, and ladies' departments'. The first floor was said to have 'very handsome showrooms for the ladies' tailoring departments'. The part of the building that extended into Gas Street housed workrooms, which combined 'every modern convenience and improvement'. In later years it became the County Cycle & Motors showroom.

Well-known architects Chamberlain & Martin designed the block in about 1875 for Joseph Sturge (see pp. 80, 81). Sturge, an anti-drinker, may not have been impressed to find that the gift-wrapped building in January 1995 was to become a pub. The pub's name, the Merchant Stores, recalls the history of the block.

The corner of Gas Street in its pre-renovation state. The early nineteenth-century buildings were extensively renovated and turned into a pub, the Tap & Spile.

A May 1990 view from the roof of the Hyatt Regency Hotel, looking down on Gas Street Basin as works continue around the chimney of the former Pearce & Cutler glassworks, which was being converted into a pub. The circular area became a fountain.

At the time of this photograph in May 1986 this short stretch of Broad Street had become a thriving antique dealers' area, centred on the Stratford House antique shop on the opposite side of the road. This view shows one of the antique and coins shops, a baker and Everyman's stationery store, which backed on to the canal basin and can be seen from above on the previous page.

The block pictured above has now been converted to leisure facilities. The main occupier is the Australian Walkabout Bar. The window sign neatly frames the buildings on the Water's Edge development on Brindleyplace. The success of the Water's Edge helped to attract other leisure developments to Broad Street.

This view, made possible by the demolition of the façade of the former Prince of Wales theatre, shows the blocks opposite the site of Bingley Hall as they looked in October 1986. The most notable occupants were the Rum Runner nightclub and the BBC. For many years Pearce & Cutler's glassworks was located here.

The Rum Runner was most famous for being the headquarters of the pop group Duran Duran who started their meteoric rise to fame there. It was said to be 'the cradle of the New Romantic movement'. Simon Le Bon, John Taylor and Nick Rhodes had a string of top ten hits, including 'Girls on Film', 'The Reflex' and 'Is There Something I Should Know?' You should know that this site is now known as Regency Wharf, a pub and restaurant complex. This leaflet dates from 1984.

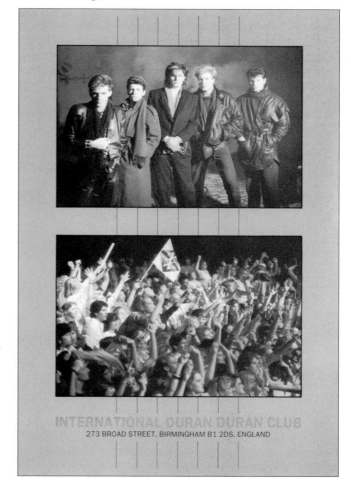

INTERNATIONAL DURAN DURAN CLUB
273 BROAD STREET, BIRMINGHAM B1 2DS, ENGLAND

The Hyatt Regency Hotel now stands on the site of these buildings, seen here in 1950. This was the headquarters and studio centre of the BBC Midlands Region until 1971. At the start of the Second World War the BBC left Broad Street for rural Evesham and returned in 1943. It was from here that the BBC first broadcast *The Archers*. The BBC expanded into Carpenter Road, Edgbaston, before moving to Pebble Mill in 1971. Stock's car supplies and Clay's musical instrument dealers are the immediate neighbours.

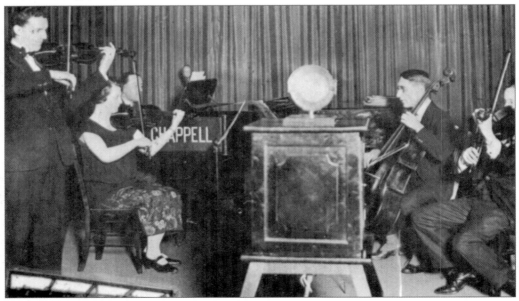

Frank Cantell and his orchestra play in the BBC studio. On the opening night it accommodated the Band of the Scots Guards, the Birmingham Station Orchestra and Full Chorus in a performance of Elgar's *The Music Makers*. Ironically, Elgar said the new phenomenon of broadcasting was 'a tin pot bastardised medium'.

The Hyatt Regency Hotel site, April 1953. The shops include Hobbs' fireplace centre on the right, and disappearing towards the city centre are Charles Williams' oil importers, Etna Glass, Jewkes' and Cooke & Murray's, a well-known surgical appliance shop.

This marvellous letterhead is from A.F. Corbett's shopfitting establishment, which stood near the junction with Bridge Street from the early 1960s until demolition. The company was established elsewhere in 1904.

H. H. MULLINER,
CARRIAGE MANUFACTURER.

BIRMINGHAM.

An assortment of New Carriages of most fashionable designs in stock at very moderate prices, including Landaus, Broughams, Victorias, Wagonettes, Phaetons, and all Description of 2-Wheel Carriages.

ALSO A NUMBER OF SOUND SECOND-HAND VEHICLES ALWAYS FOR SALE.

Men sent to examine Carriages requiring Repairs, and Estimates supplied without charge.

CARRIAGES INSURED AGAINST ACCIDENTS.

Show Rooms: 300 & 301, BROAD STREET

WORKS: 10, 11 & 12, GAS STREET.

BIRMINGHAM.

Transglobe travel agents stood near the corner with Bridge Street throughout the 1950s and early 1960s. Here we see the winner of the Miss Paris competition, Pat Wood, accepting her prize from Joseph Shutz. Later still this was the home of the Rendezvous café, which provided competition for the nearby Appolonia café.

Mulliner's had showrooms on Broad Street until about 1915. The advertisement dates from 1888 when the company was said to have been the first to offer insurance of their carriages against accidents 'at very moderate rates, considering the risks undertaken'. Later Mulliner's built motor car bodies.

A Second World War photograph showing the bombed remains of Bridge Street. Baskerville House, with its air raid precaution building on the roof, is in the background.

Cadbury's chocolate makers began in the town centre in 1824 but expanded to premises on Bridge Street in 1847 to take advantage of the canal, and it was, at that time at least, away from 'uliginous [sooty] quarter, on the verge of Edgbaston – that Belgravia of Birmingham – where sunshine and blue sky are not perpetually hidden by smoke'. Both the business and the town rapidly expanded and Cadbury made the decision to move out to the countryside and build 'a factory in a garden' at Bournville. This sketch, possibly drawn with a little artistic licence, is taken from an old billhead and shows the factory yard. The Bridge Street premises later became a school, which moved to Oozells Street in 1898.

Work is under way to construct the 24-storey 319-room Hyatt Regency Hotel overlooking Gas Street canal basin. The hotel is the city's third tallest building, and is clad in 8,500 m² of reflective glass panels, which is quite appropriate as it is built on land that was once occupied by glass merchants Pearce & Cutler, Arculus and Etna. Originally a triangular hotel was envisaged, but plans were altered and the rectangular hotel was built slightly further back from Broad Street than first planned. No one, it seems, told the planners: the bridge to the ICC was slightly too short when it was erected in 1989 and an additional piece was added! The canal stops to the right at Bridge Street, but originally went under the road into a two-pronged basin where the large flat-roofed building now stands. At that time this was Central Television headquarters.

The statue of three famous people who helped shape Birmingham's history stands outside the Register Office. The office, a former college, is where local people go to register births, deaths and marriages, though not necessarily in that order. The threesome is Matthew Boulton (1728–1809), James Watt (1736–1819), who developed steam engines to produce power, and William Murdoch (1754–1839), who invented gas lighting. The memorial was unveiled in 1956.

This 1953 view shows the Masonic building, erected following a design competition in 1927. The foundation stone ceremony was performed a mile away in front of an audience of Masons at their headquarters in Corporation Street! The event was synchronised by electric control, which signalled the raising and lowering of cranes to which the stone was attached, thus continuing the secrecy that surrounds their activities. The building, which features a stone frieze on the façade, was erected as a memorial to those Masons who fell in the First World War. In 1962 it became an engineering building centre, and was briefly occupied by Central Television.

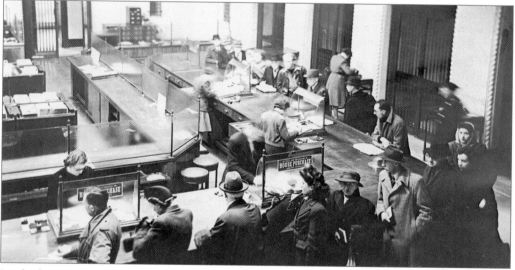

Inside the Birmingham Municipal Bank, which later became the TSB. This was the first municipal savings bank in the country, and was originally intended to help the First World War effort by promoting savings, but it became very successful and was made permanent. At the end of the first twenty months 30,000 people had deposited £500,000; 80 per cent of them agreed to lend their money to the government. This building dates from 1932, when the Rt Hon. Neville Chamberlain, who originally conceived the idea and became the first chairman, laid the foundation stone.

The 302 ft high office block, Alpha Tower, reflected in the glass of the Hyatt Regency Hotel. It is part of a 1970 development, which incorporated studios for the regional ITV company then called ATV. It was to be called Paradise Tower, but a competition was held instead for members of the public to suggest the name. One person suggested it should be called 'Shirtsleeves', simply because it had the letters ITV in it! That suggestion was not taken up, and it became Alpha Tower after the Alpha Studios in Aston where the TV station was previously located.

In 1902 two entrepreneurs by the names of Robert Lee and George Longland took over the cabinet-making business of Gaunt & Co., and the business they founded is now the longest surviving concern on Broad Street. This is the premises as it looked in 1930 shortly before they moved further along Broad Street. The first stock book dates from July 1903: it is recorded that a cabinet had been purchased from Banbury and sold for £1 15s 0d.

Lee Longland's cabinet works at the back of the building, leading on to an arm of the canal. Timber arrived by canal and was taken directly into the workshops.

Lee Longland's first motorised van, which dates from 1912. The early distribution was carried out by horse-drawn van.

The congested canalside scene as it looked in a sketch drawn in the 1890s. An 1845 directory indicates that there were fifty-five coal merchants at the Old Wharf. The first consignment of coal was unloaded there in 1769. The grounds of Bingley House are still resisting the relentless advance of urban sprawl. Notice also the large canal offices, which are at the end of the forked canal basin. These are pictured below.

The imposing entrance to the Old Wharf as it looked from Paradise Row.

These impressive offices, belonging to an assurance company, stood on the corner of Broad Street and Easy Row. They were built overlooking the Old Wharf and later joined up with the canal offices. On the other side of the offices stood an entertainment venue, known as Curzon Hall. Nearby stood the residence of Mr Winkle, the wharfinger (wharf manager) mentioned in *The Pickwick Papers*.

A bill was passed in 1926 to effect the closure of the Old Wharf, and after the canals were filled in the land became a car park for 600 cars. The local press reported: 'When the Old Wharf is ready as a car park Birmingham will be one of the few cities in England where the municipality has directly made provision for this growing need of communal life.' It added: 'A charge will, of course, be made for the privilege of leaving a car, and there is little doubt that a substantial revenue will accrue.' The charges were 1s 6d for the whole day or 1s for part of the day. This photograph was taken in October 1931.

Acknowledgements

I would like to thank the following people and organisations for either supplying information or photographs for this book:

Richard Albutt, Jennifer Archer, Patrick Baird, Frank Bartlam, Nora Bartlam, Alan Chatham, Carl Chinn, Ian Cox, Eileen Doyle, Kathleen Elliott, Margery Elliott, June Felton, John Gale, Ken Hughes, William Jeavons, Juliet Jordan, Pete Judd, John Landon, Margaret Lee, Gareth Lewis, Ian MacKenzie, Scott O'Hara, Jack Powell, Barbara Reynolds (née Beeny), Roy Schutz, Anthony Spettigue, Gary Taylor, Chris Upton, Vicki Valsecchi, Bert Wilkes, Birmingham City Council, Central Library Local Studies and History Department, Photographic Section, NEC Group ICC Archive, BBCTV Public Relations Department, T.S. Vernon Archive, Bass Brewery Archive, Brindleyplace Archive and *Birmingham Evening Mail*.

In celebration of Birmingham's canal heritage, these people dressed up in appropriate outfits for the occasion. They are seen on the canal arm near the Longboat pub.